women-at work

From A Dining Room Table... To A Million Dollar Institution

A Pictorial Overview

WOMEN IN SUPPORT OF THE MILLION MAN MARCH, INC.

Copyright 2005 by WISOMMM, Inc.

Cover and Internal Design by Yvonne Onque

Photo Credits
All photos by William Frazier, Sulaiman Onque, Yusef Ismail
Some photos by permission of the Newark Star Ledger

Special thanks to Allied Printing
973-227-0520

All rights reserved. No part of this book may be reproduced in any form without prior permission by the publisher.

Published by
Women In Support of the Million Man March, Inc.
53 Lincoln Park, Newark, NJ 07102
Phone: 973-297-1275
Fax: 973-297-1120
www.wisommm.org

First and foremost, the Women In Support Of the Million Man March would like to give honor to The Divine Creator of all things, without whom nothing is possible. We are eternally grateful for all of our blessings and continue to pray that we are kept strong and unified as we strive toward what is right.

WISOMMM would also like to thank the Ancestors, for without their guidance, we would surely be lost. We believe that the Spirit of the Ancestors are with us and we pray that they are proud of what we put forth.

We would like to thank The Honorable Minister Louis Farrakhan, whom God chose to speak through when he called the historic Million Man March on October 16, 1995. We thank him for his leadership, love and support.

We thank the brothers and sisters of the African community. We know that regardless of our geographical location, religious affiliation or social background, we are one people. It has been your generosity and commitment that has helped sustained us through the years. We salute you all.

WISOMMM expresses our special thanks to the following people and organizations for their loving support:

Hon. Sharpe James, Mayor - Newark, NJ & NJ State Senator
Newark Municipal Council & The City of Newark, NJ
Sy Henderson, Financial Consultant
DeLacy Davis & Black Cops Against Police Brutality
Muhammad's Mosque #25 - Newark, New Jersey
Faheem Ra'Oof-CPA, Yeadon & Ra'Oof
The Nation of Islam
Senators Jon Corzine & Frank Lautenberg
Pamela Anderson, NJ Economic Development Authority
Senator Wynona Lipman (Ancestor)
Independence Community Bank
Newark Public Schools, Office of Early Childhood
Girl Scouts of Greater Essex & Hudson
Newark Teachers Association
The Brothers of Integrity & Port House
Malik Akbar, Sheffield Electrical
Curtis Morrow
Interfaith Ministries Productions
Sulaiman Onque, Artist
Samad Onque, Artist
Philip Thomas, Performing Arts Services
Faheem Salaam
Sister Claudette Marie Muhammad, Nation of Islam
Huriyyah and Rahjan Nassiruddin
David and Shikhana Muhammad

Rayford Scott, Kindle & Scott Contractors
Dr. Adelaide Sanford, Advisory Board
Drs. Leonard & Rosalind Jeffries, Advisory Board
Betty Dobson & Dr. James McIntosh, CEMOTAP
William Frazier Photographer & WISOMMM Advisory Board
John Howard, Howard Security Plus
Minister Louis Farrakhan, Nation of Islam
Audrey West (Ancestor)
Raisah Myers, Advisory Board
Lisa Richardson, Esq.
Ted Williams, Alzra Design Group
Larry Lawson, City of Newark
Councilwoman Patricia Perkins-Auguste, Advisory Board
Newark Pre-School Council
Johnny Thomas, Upholstery Plus, Inc.
Bruce Jones, Fleet Heat Express
Henry Samedy, Triune Productions
Richard Smith, Cablevision
Nassar Ameen, Cable TV Technician
Linda Jones-Bell, Cable TV Technician
Saadiq Shakoor
Carol Cleveland, Newark Public Schools
Haqqa and Tayyiba Aziz
Akbar Salaam, Unity Beef
Tamika Riley, TRI Inc.

All of the dedicated teachers and aides at the WISOMMM Holistic Child Care Center
Lynette France, Amelia Rocto-James, Karima Leggett-Onque, Lakisha McMillan, Yusef Ismail, Claudette Batson, Cynthia Howard, Akiba Ismail, Crystal Williams, Shaleata Howard, Rosalind O'Neal, Aleida Mena, Rafael Mena, Sajdah Samuels, Rachel Brooks, Maria Santos, Tiffany Perkins, Nastassia Little, Dionna Walker, Fatima Finney, and to all of the parents and generous people who have volunteered their valuable time and resources.

In loving memory of Queen Mother Rosa Parks (1913 - 2005)

Dedication by Dr. Rosalind Jeffries

WISOMMM is an activist community education group that functions out of an historic unique five building complex. This collective of women was born out of crisis, a forced response as conscious mothers and sisters determined to take a firm stance to build for the future, even if it was in the face of death. Their determination follows the ancient traditions of organic healing, goal orientation, and educational upliftment. This belief parallels the ancestral format that was entitled, Kongolo, the spirit of the group that is greater than any individual component part. This concept was brought over from monotheistic Central Afrika and constituted the circle of people within the square known as Kongo Square, in New Orleans. From such portals in slavery, and post slavery, Black people from Afrika and the Caribbean were dispersed throughout the U.S. WISOMMM resurrected that power circle supporting men and children. Women In Support Of the Million Man March will gather at the Washington, D.C. obelisk/tekhen, theoretically the same Kongolo circle. Impetus for resurrection was the suffering of masses, aggression, disunity, therefore, the ancestors at Kongo Square did not discriminate according to the richness of ethnic origin, or religion, Islam, Christian, Buddhism, or traditional African religion. The cooperative collective, communal in sharp focus dictated one Supreme Being who was evident by 1) making the impossible possible, 2) operational in the greatness of continued creation, 3) Beauty, Grace and Splendor.

WISOMMM does not uphold discrimination, falsely evaluating various denominations, or ethnicities, but rather seeking the common denominator to pursue that strong moral fiber upon which nations can stand. Resurrection of the neglected brings vital force as an expression of creativity, and that is anti-death. It brings flexibility, the hallmark of healthy, imagination, and vision. It brings fertility that develops the immune system with morals, self-esteem, and family. Maat is the Kemetic principle of Mother/Sister in balance with men and children, harmony, and reciprocity. Historically, women who rose to support in crisis included: Harriet Tubman, the foundation of the established Freedom Schools after the Civil War; Ida B. Wells, Journalist, leader in the campaign against lynching of men and children; reaction to the massive deaths in Tulsa, Oklahoma 1921, and Rosewood 1923, the anti-violence move was to benefit all of the ethnic, and racial groups of America; the school of Mary McLeod Bethune; and the role that Rosa Parks played, the spark of the Martin Luther King Civil Rights Movement for basic Human Rights. Women supported that movement. Afrikan American history is imperative. Too many still view us from negative media stereotype. The correct teaching and schooling is an aim of WISOMMM. We must salute those who move independently motivated by the need to balance truth, giving correct love. Your love must take up these greater causes by sacrificing your financial support and praying collectively for the masses. To financially support a worthy group is to save yourself in these most unusual times. It must not be said that in a time of absolutes in cultural pollution and natural catastrophes you did not make a sacrifice beyond the biases of denominationalism in order to rescue the perishing and push humanity to gain higher heights.

Foreword

by Dr. Leonard J. Jeffries

We are all extremely proud of the achievements of the Women In Support Of the Million Man March (WISOMMM) and are deeply indebted to them for their vision, their motivation and their concrete historic accomplishments. They have provided us with a national and international model of how we can plan together, build together and leave a lasting legacy for our children and their children. Inspired by the call of Minister Louis Farrakhan ten years ago to mobilize and organize our local and national communities for self-development following the program outlined earlier by the Honorable Elijah Muhammad, these spirit-filled women of Greater Newark have established the most significant example in the nation of grassroots collective building for eternity.

The WISOMMM institutions at Lincoln Park have provided the community with excellent educational and cultural facilities. The recently purchased historic landmark complex of three-buildings at Washington Park in the heart of Newark, New Jersey's downtown cultural community has allowed these dedicated women to establish the much needed African Education and Cultural Resource Center (AECRC). This 65,000 square foot facility houses a beautiful sanctuary, two large auditoriums, fellowship hall, gymnasium, bowling alley, and a five-story school building with many classrooms. This complex will give WISOMMM the space to expand so that it can carry out its sacred mission to help restore and develop the African American community. It will be the centerpiece of the Village where programs and processes of renewal and redevelopment can take place. It is often said that it takes an entire village to raise a child. WISOMMM offers the Greater Newark community a unique center that allows the urban village to mobilize its resources, galvanize its expertise, target its special problems so that it can be a National Model of Group and Community Development. This Model will help create and implement educational designs that bring out the genius in our children. It will prepare motivational processes that open up a pathway of success to higher education. It will establish a much needed formula to allow our young men and women to find the ability to positively resocialize and acculturate in order to contribute to the community after incarceration. This historic and unique urban village center will attract families that need healing and repair and help institutions and organizations find the ability to refine their missions and make them accountable to the people. We are all thankful that the Mayor of Newark, NJ, the Honorable Sharpe James, and the City Council of Newark, particularly the Honorable Gayle Chaneyfield-Jenkins, Councilwoman-at-Large, were able to appreciate the vision and mission of WISOMMM and provide the critical support needed to compliment the assistance of the Newark Presbytery and the banks.

The Women In Support Of the Million Man March have clearly shown us the path to individual, family, community and national restoration and redevelopment. We are truly blessed to have this example before us. It should be studied, analyzed and assessed so that it can become part of a Greater Empowerment of our People. Their work in response to the call to renewed greatness by Minister Farrakhan has put in our hands a proven Blueprint for African American success and triumph. Our responsibility is to replicate and duplicate and make it a key to the cultural renewal of our people. Their work is part of the Great Awakening of a strategic segment of our Global Community. We must support their efforts in every way possible. They represent the Best of our Legacy of Struggle and Victory against insurmountable odds. We must be able to benefit from the WISOMMM example. Our hope is that the Millions More Movement will be emboldened by this proven example of the rewards of self-development, the power of organization, the benefits of perseverance, the fruit of vision and the results of a Blessed Sacred Mission.

An Overview

WOMEN IN SUPPORT OF THE MILLION MAN MARCH

Women In Support Of the Million Man March, Inc. (WISOMMM) is a non-profit community based organization, based in Newark, New Jersey, and born out of the Million Man March, which took place in Washington, D.C. on October 16, 1995. WISOMMM was originally formed to be a women's contingent and a means of support for the March. The sisters sold t-shirts throughout the state that touted "Women In Support Of the Million Man March - we've got your back"! WISOMMM used the money raised to purchase buses to go to Washington, D.C. While registering men for the March, the Sisters also registered thousands of men and women to vote. WISOMMM, along with the Statewide and Local Organizing Committees, helped send over 50,000 men from the State of new Jersey to the Million Man March.

The women of WISOMMM vowed to continue the spirit and momentum they had achieved during the march and to recommit themselves to serving the community according to the tenets of the Million Man March which include faith, empowerment, self-love, self-determination, and reunification of the family. Although the organization is comprised of a diverse group of women from various religious, cultural and social backgrounds, WISOMMM has always had one goal - to improve the lives of people of African descent through community service, cultural enrichment, education, social activism and economic empowerment.

In November of 1995 WISOMMM was incorporated. The organization has a governing body and Executive Staff of twenty-one (21) members, and a nine (9) member Advisory Board. Fredrica Bey, who coordinated WISOMMM and has been its Executive Director since its inception, realized that the first thing the organization needed was a headquarters. After two years of meeting in Sister Bey's home and sitting at her dining room table, she began to search for a more permanent base of operations. Being a licensed Realtor, Sister Bey easily found WISOMMM a home.

53 Lincoln Park, a mansion in Newark's historic Lincoln Park Arts District is an 18th Century Victorian Home registered with the New Jersey Historical Society as a Historical Landmark. The Sisters of WISOMMM quickly went to work raising money to buy this gem. Whether it was sponsoring a fish fry or collecting pennies in the park, WISOMMM was determined to purchase this property. In January 1997, the organization purchased its current headquarters, now known as WISOMMM Mansion. In August 2001, WISOMMM purchased another historical Newark Mansion, 67-69 Lincoln Park.

Organizations who currently call WISOMMM Mansions I and II home are the Girl Scouts of Greater Essex and Hudson Counties, the Newark Teachers Association, S.T.E.P. Program (Striving Together Equals Progress - a rites of passage program for young men) and the Newark New Jersey Chapter of Sister's Network - a national breast cancer survivor's support organization for African American Women.

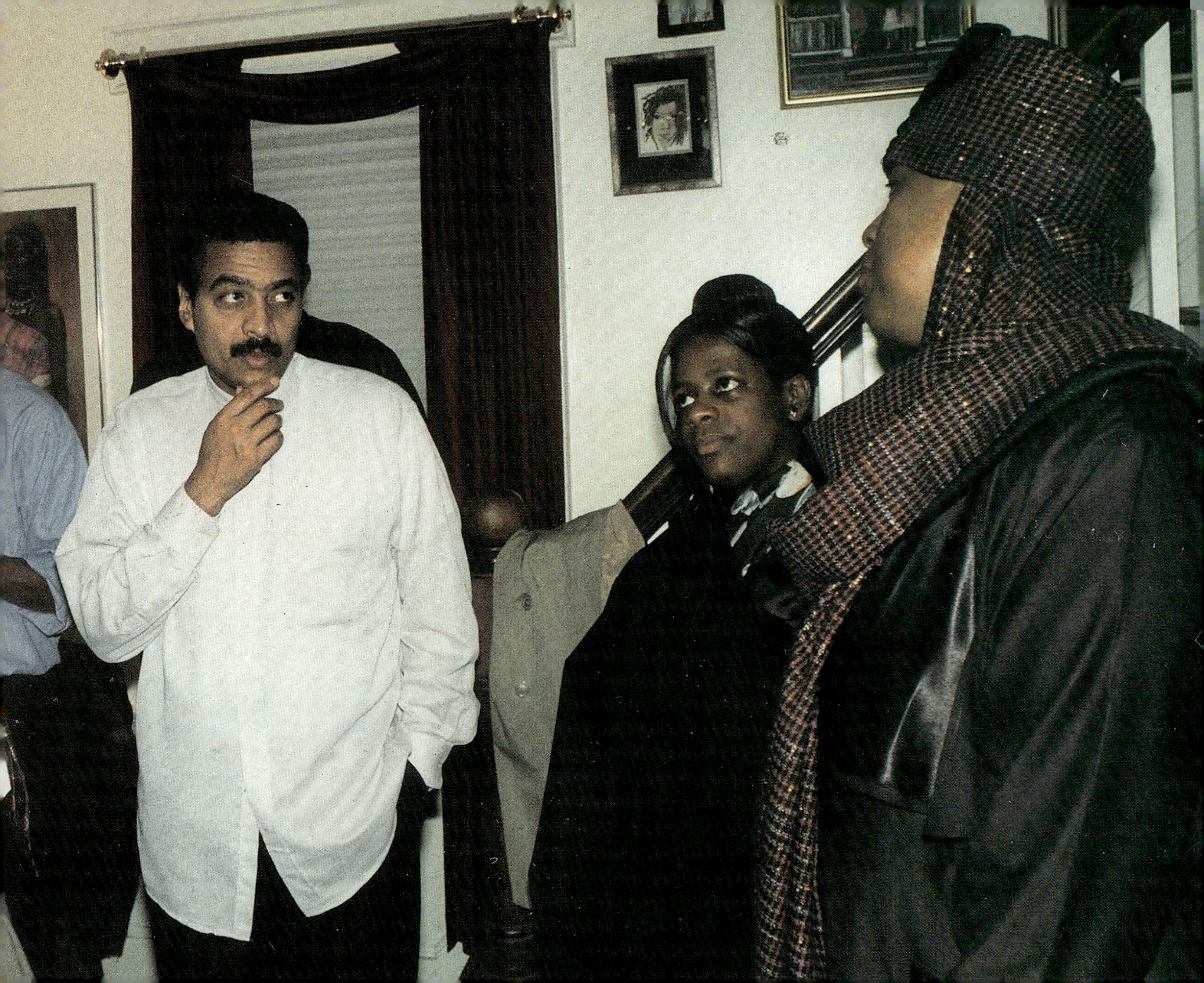

An Organization is Born

On a warm August evening in Newark, New Jersey the first meeting to the New Jersey Million Man March Coalition was held at Ruben's Restaurant, a local supper club owned by entrepreneur Ruben Johnson and attorney Bill Manns. The coalition was co-chaired by Minister Khadir Muhammad of Mosque #25 and Lawrence Hamm of the People's Organization for Progress. Emphasis was on "liberation through unity" and so it was quite natural to include the women in the effort to organize for the march.

"There was something about that first meeting that spoke to the magnitude of the march, not only for New Jersey but for an entire nation of people. We could hardly imagine how huge this was going to be."

Fredrica Bey, Executive Director
Women In Support of the Million Man March, Inc.

Pictured Left: New Jersey State Wide Chairman Lawrence Hamm, Councilwoman Patricia Perkins-Auguste and Fredrica Bey, Executive Director of Women In Support of the Million Man March discuss mobilizing strategies for the 1995 Million Man March.

Pictured Right: Co-Chairs Minister Kadir Muhammad and Sister Cathy Muhammad of the Nation of Islam and Lawrence Hamm preside over a mobilization meeting.

CHOOSING A LEADER

In August, 1995 Sister Fredrica Bey was appointed chairwoman of the Women In Support of the Million Man March.

She later became Executive Director and incorporated the organization with tax exempt status.

Pictured Left: Sister Fredrica Bey address a group of men, encouraging them to attend the 1995 Million Man March.

Pictured Right: Executive Board Member Bonita Satterfield rallies for support for the march.

WOMEN IN SUPPORT

OF THE MILLION MAN MARCH

traveled throughout the State raising funds and registering many of the 50,000 men from New Jersey who attended the historical march.

FINDING A HOME...

As Executive Director of WISOMMM, Fredrica Bey realized that the first thing the organization needed was a headquarters. After two years of meeting in Sister Bey's home and sitting at her dinning room table, she began the search for a more permanent base of operations. Being a licensed Realtor made it easy to find WISOMMM a home.

Pictured Left: Using over twenty years of experience as a real estate agent, Fredrica Bey examines a potential headquarters for her newly formulated organization.

Pictured Right: Fredrica Bey holds a press conference announcing the women's intentions to purchase the mansion at 53 Lincoln Park in Newark

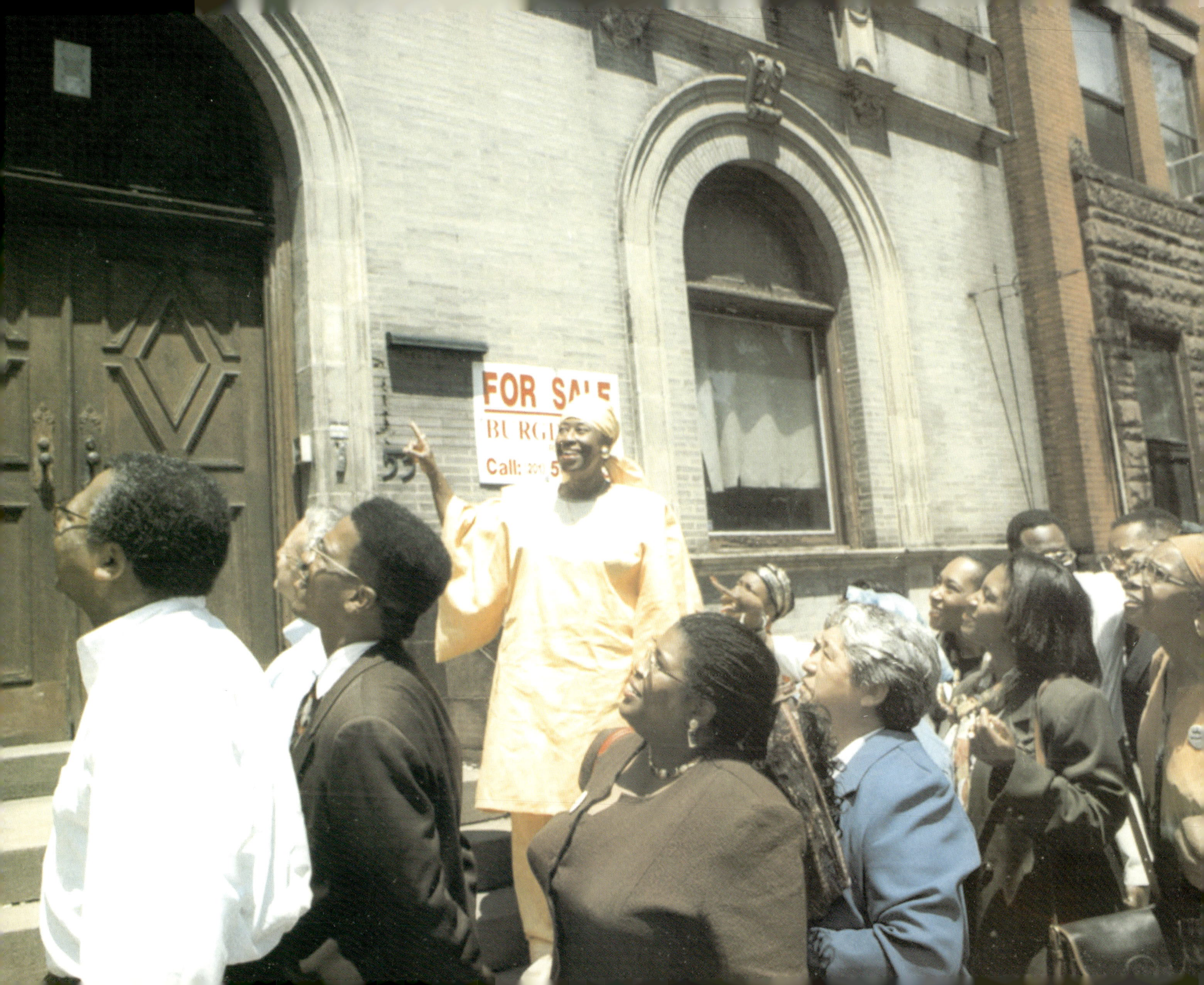
FOR SALE
Call:

53 Lincoln Park, a mansion in Newark's historic Lincoln Park Arts District is an 18th Century Victorian Home registered with the New Jersey Historical Society as a Historical Landmark. The Sisters of WISOMMM quickly went to work raising money to buy this gem. Whether it was sponsoring a fish fry or collecting pennies in the park, the women of WISOMMM were determined to purchase this property. In January 1997, the organization did purchase its current headquarters, now known as the WISOMMM Mansion.

ANOTHER ONE... WHY NOT?

In August 2001, WISOMMM purchased another historical Newark Mansion, 67-69 Lincoln Park.

Both mansions are used to operate programs and provide commercial space for other local organizations.

Pictured Left: The WISOMMM Mansion

Pictured Right: WISOMMM Mansion II

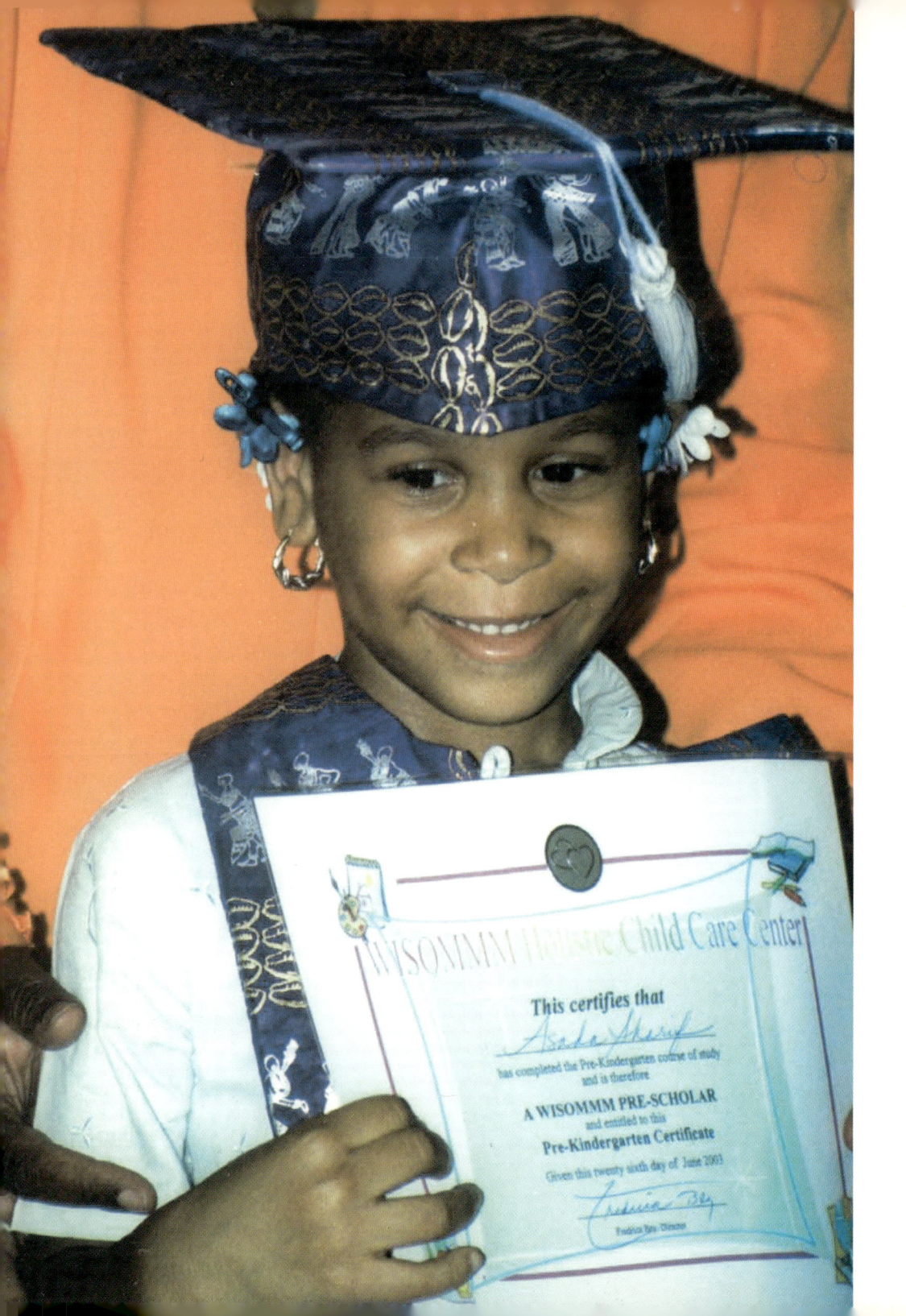

TEACHING FUTURE LEADERS

On September 10, 2001, just one day before the 9/11 disaster WISOMMM successfully opened its state-of-the-art childcare center under the guidance of Head Start and the Newark Public School District.

The WISOMMM Holistic Child Care Center provides a nurturing and educational environment for 3 and 4 year olds. Like its organization, WISOMMM's Child Care Center, has a spiritual center. Children are taught not only the basics in academics, but are placed on the path of self-discovery. Learning who they are and where they come from is an essential part the child care experience.

Pictured Left: A WISOMMM "Pre-Scholar" proudly displays her Certificate of Completion and officially moves on to Kindergarten.

Pictured Right: WISOMMM children enjoy the WISOMMM Children's Garden in front of the Ancestral Sacred Wall.

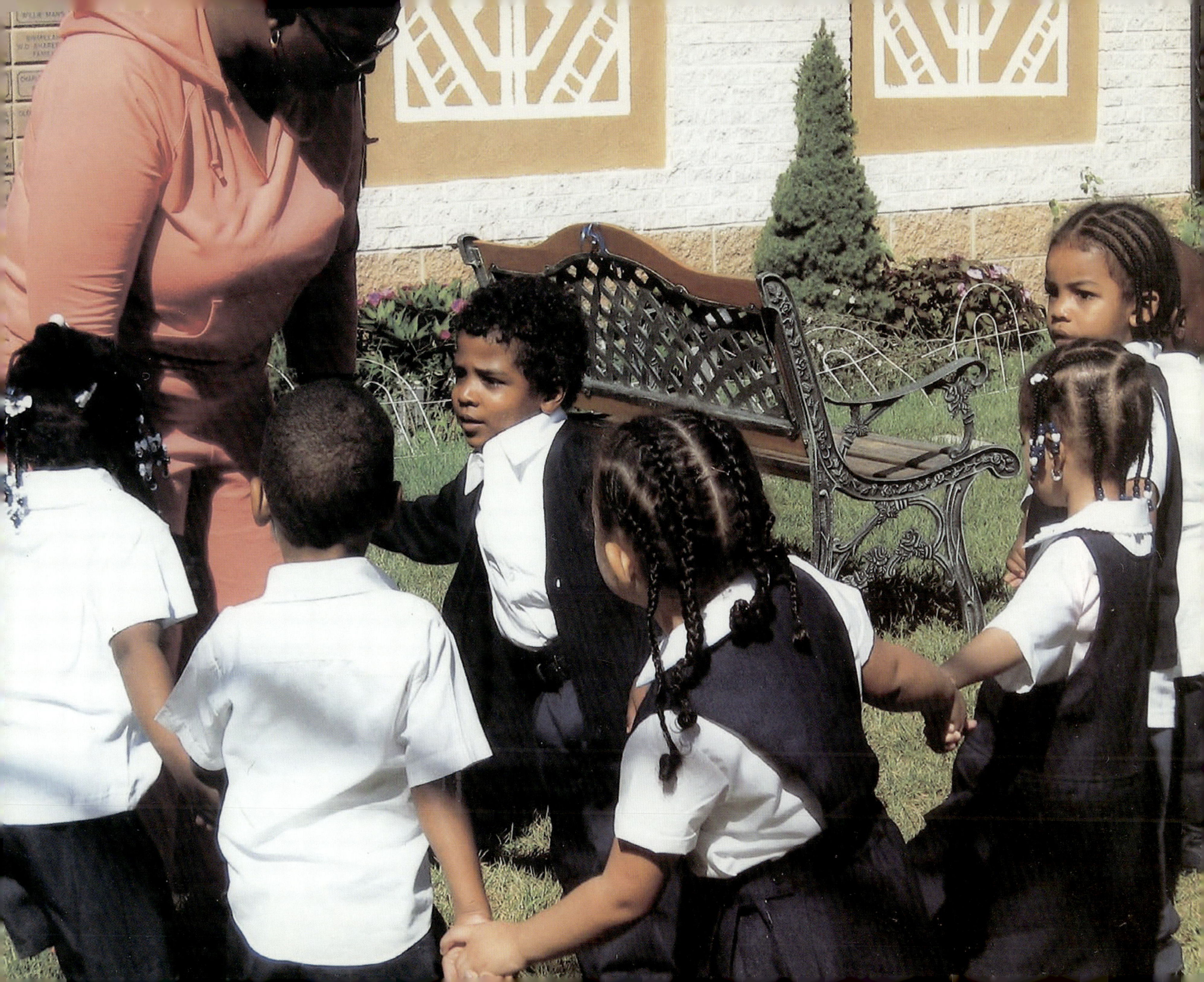

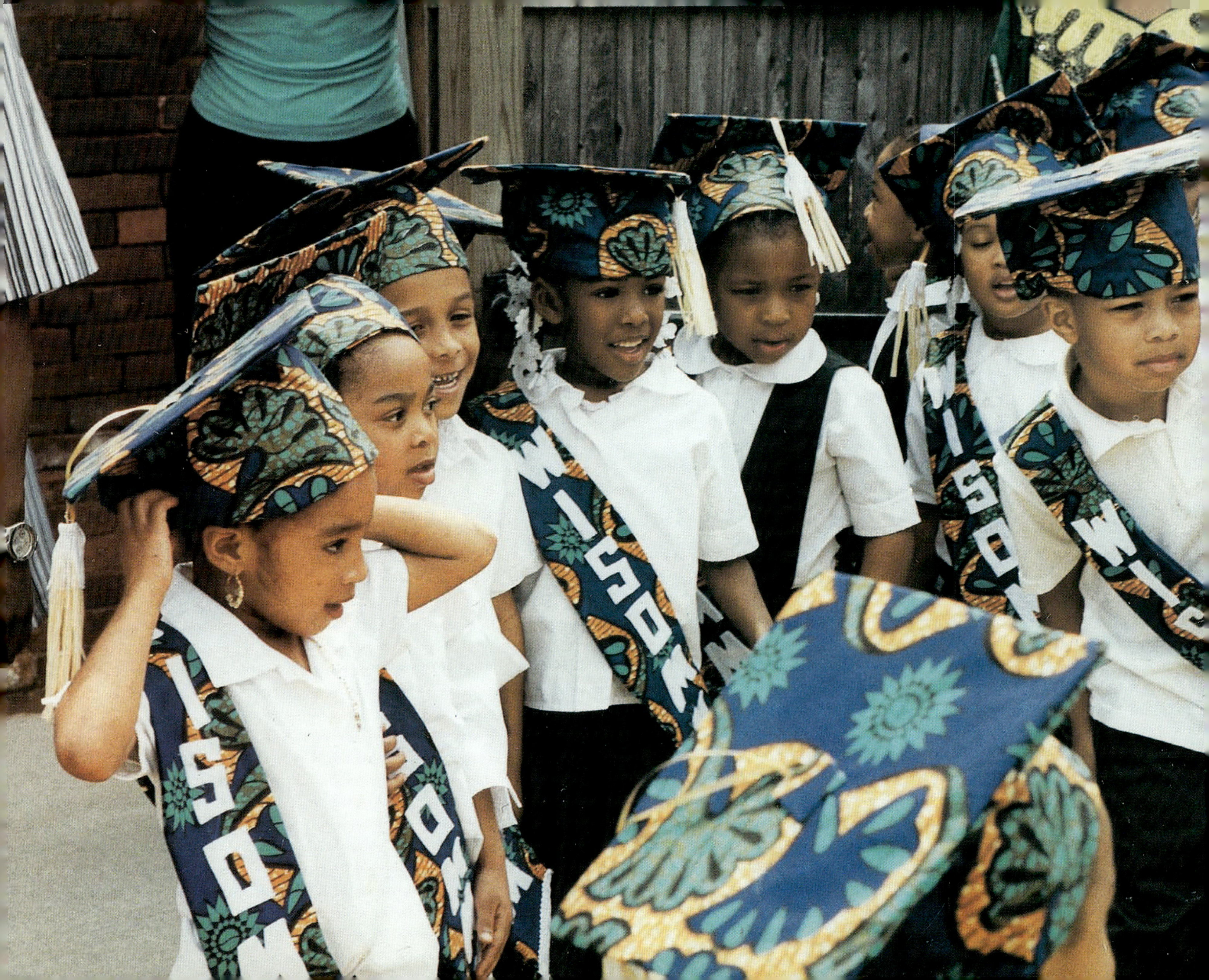
WISDOM

SENDING THEM OFF

Each year in June the WISOMMM "Pre-Scholars" successfully complete the educational journey at the WISOMMM Holistic Child Care Center, all ready to meet their next challenge. Many of the children are sad to leave.

Pictured Left: WISOMMM "Pre-Scholars" prepare themselves for the grand Send Off Celebration.

Pictured Right: Fredrica Bey consoles Shondre Peek who is reluctant to say goodbye. Shondre and his sister Keyarra were both enrolled in The WISOMMM Holistic Child Care Center whlie their mother served active duty with the US military in Afghanistan.

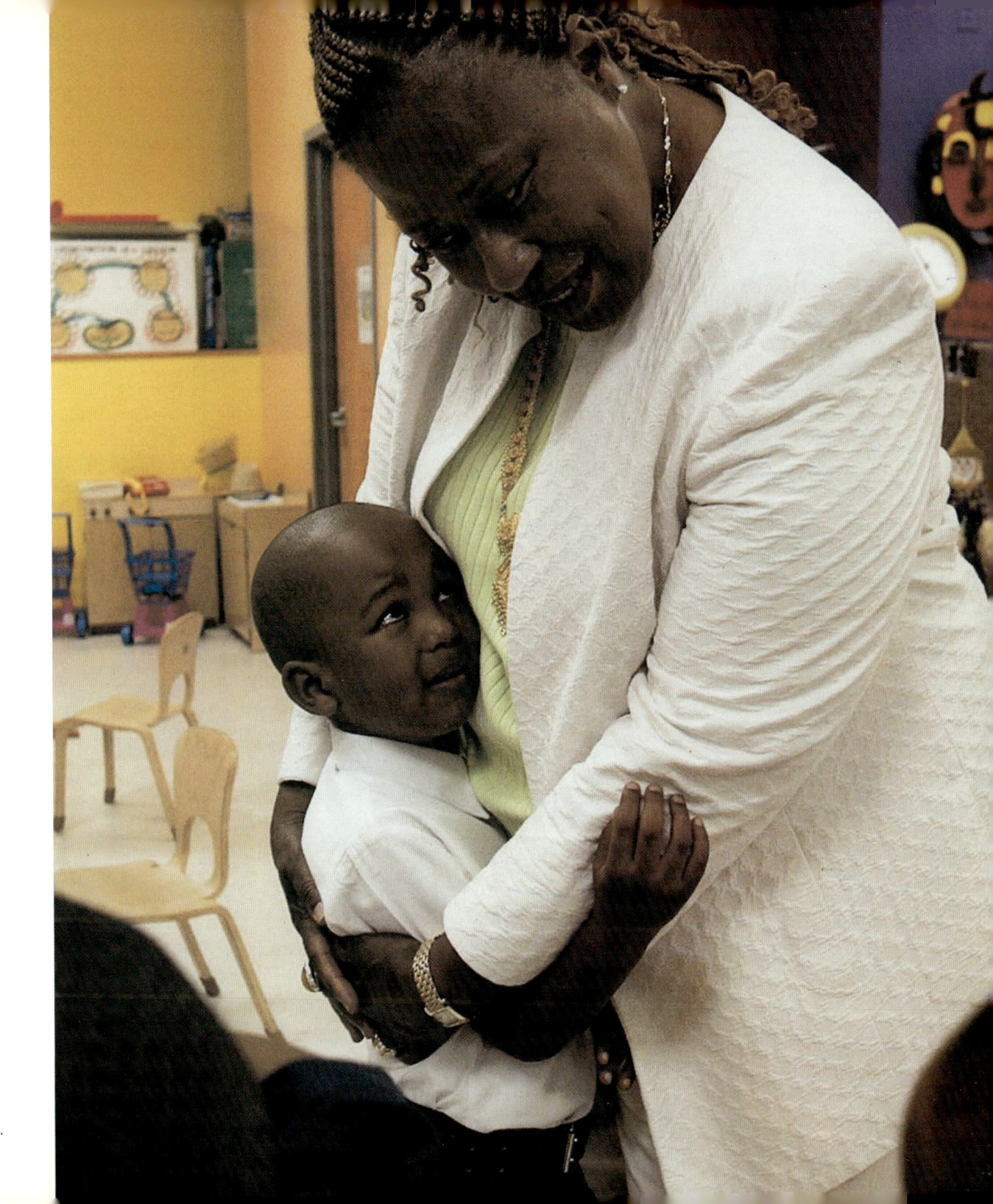

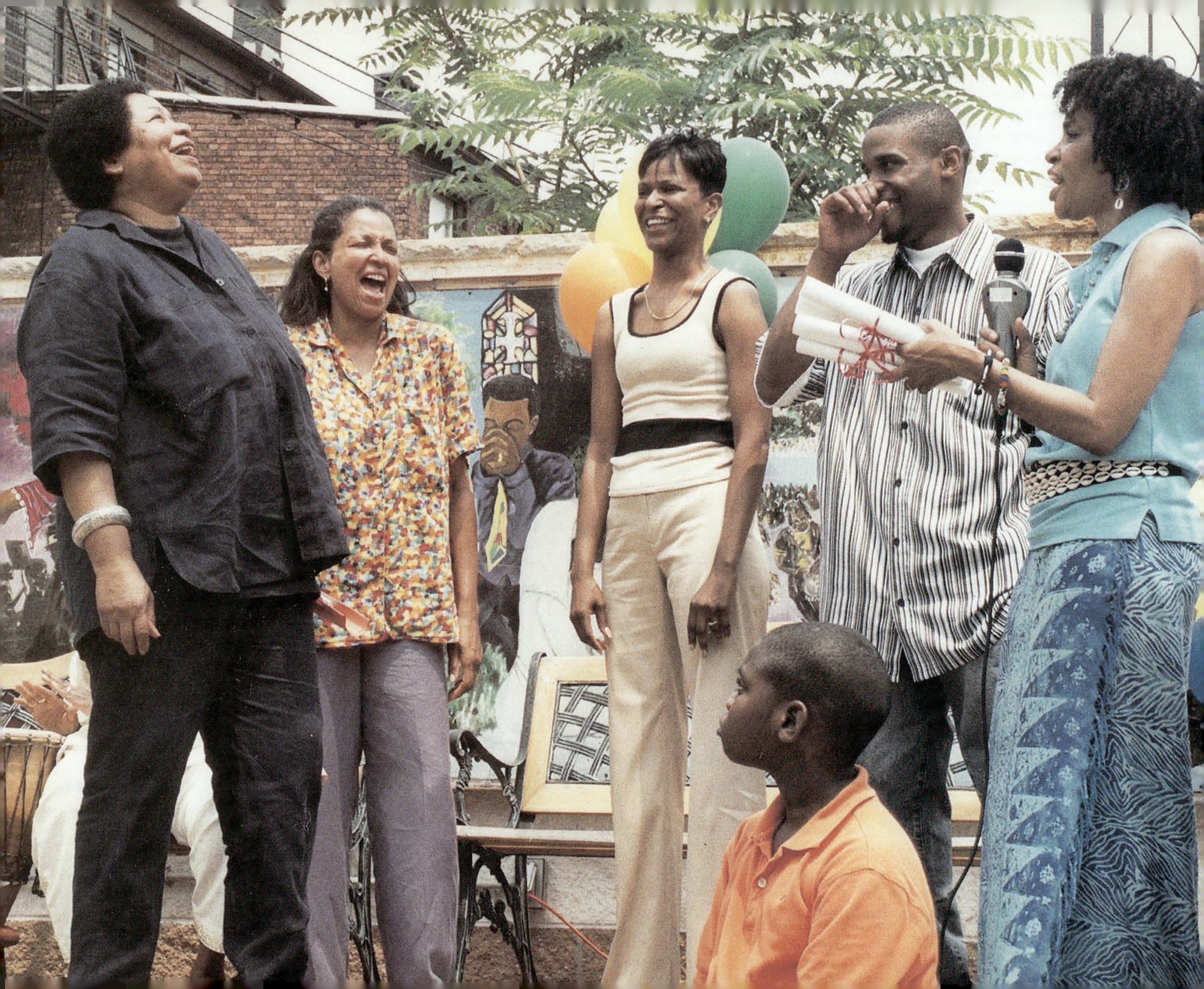

The "Send Off" celebration gives WISOMMM teachers and families the perfect opportunity to honor our children's accomplishments.

The teaching staff at the WISOMMM Holistic Child Care Center works diligently thoughout the school year to ensure that all expectations of the age-appropriate curriculum are met. Once that is achieved the educational experience is further enriched with an innovative and creative curriculum which includes science, geography, social studies, language arts and mathematics.

Pictured Left: Staff members of the child care center are awarded certificates of appreciation by Executive Board member Yvonne Onque.

Pictured Right: A WISOMMM Pre-Scholar recites excerpts from Dr. Martin Luther King, Jr's "I Have A Dream" speech at the fourth annual Send Off celebration.

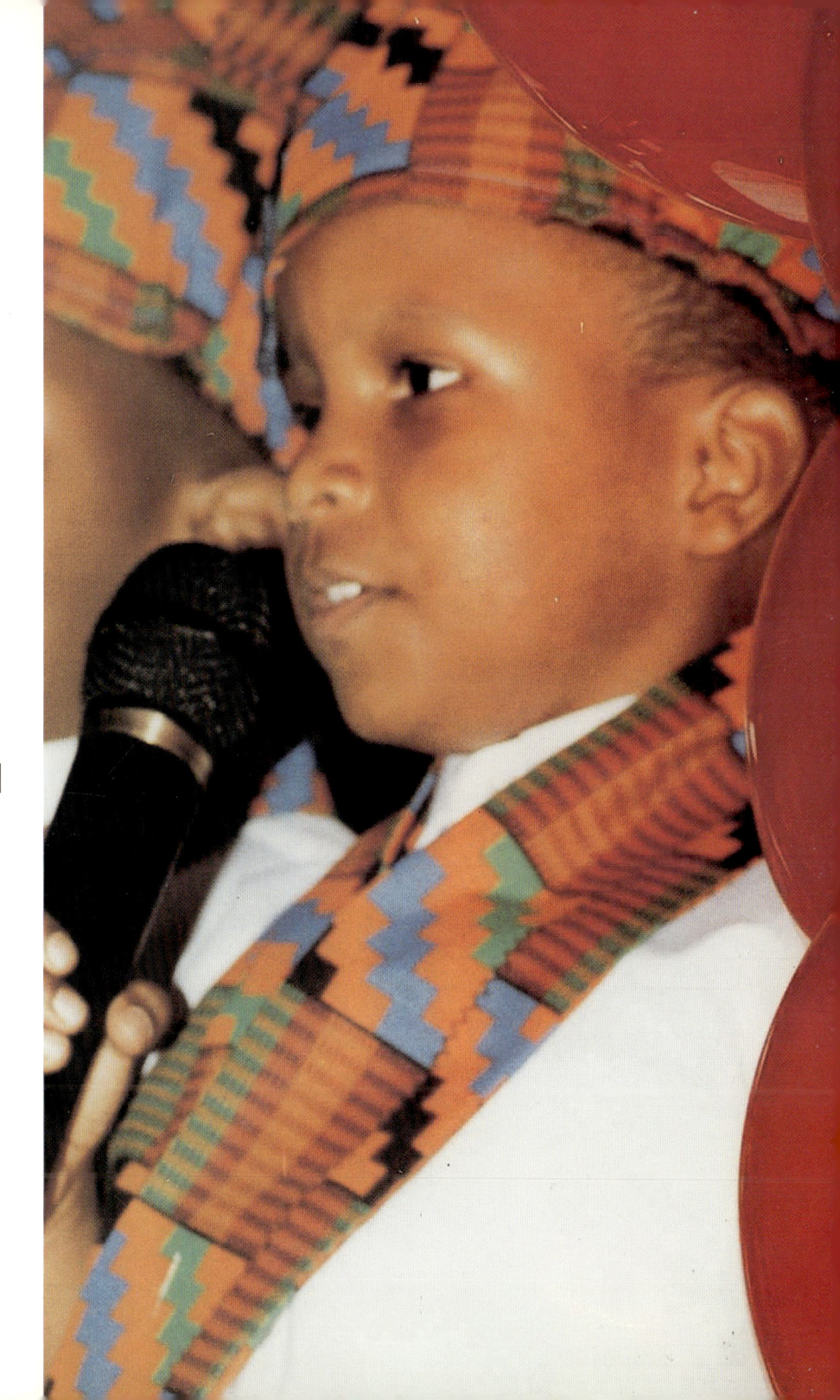

CELEBRATING MOTHERS

Each year WISOMMM honors our mothers at a Pre-Mother's Day Brunch Cruise.

While sailing around the New York, New Jersey harbor, mothers dine and dance in the finest fashion.

Pictured Left: Julia Douglas, a strong supporter of WISOMMM enjoys the Pre-Mother's Day Brunch Cruise.

The Women of WISOMMM try never to miss an opportunity to raise much needed funds. Over the past ten years much of WISOMMM's success is due to the community's willingness to participate in on-going fund raisers. A fundamental example of *Ujaama* (coopertive economics).

Pictured Left: *Board member Ayo McMillian and general member Cynthia Howard count out tickets for a 50-50 raffle on the Pre-Mother's Day Brunch Cruise.*

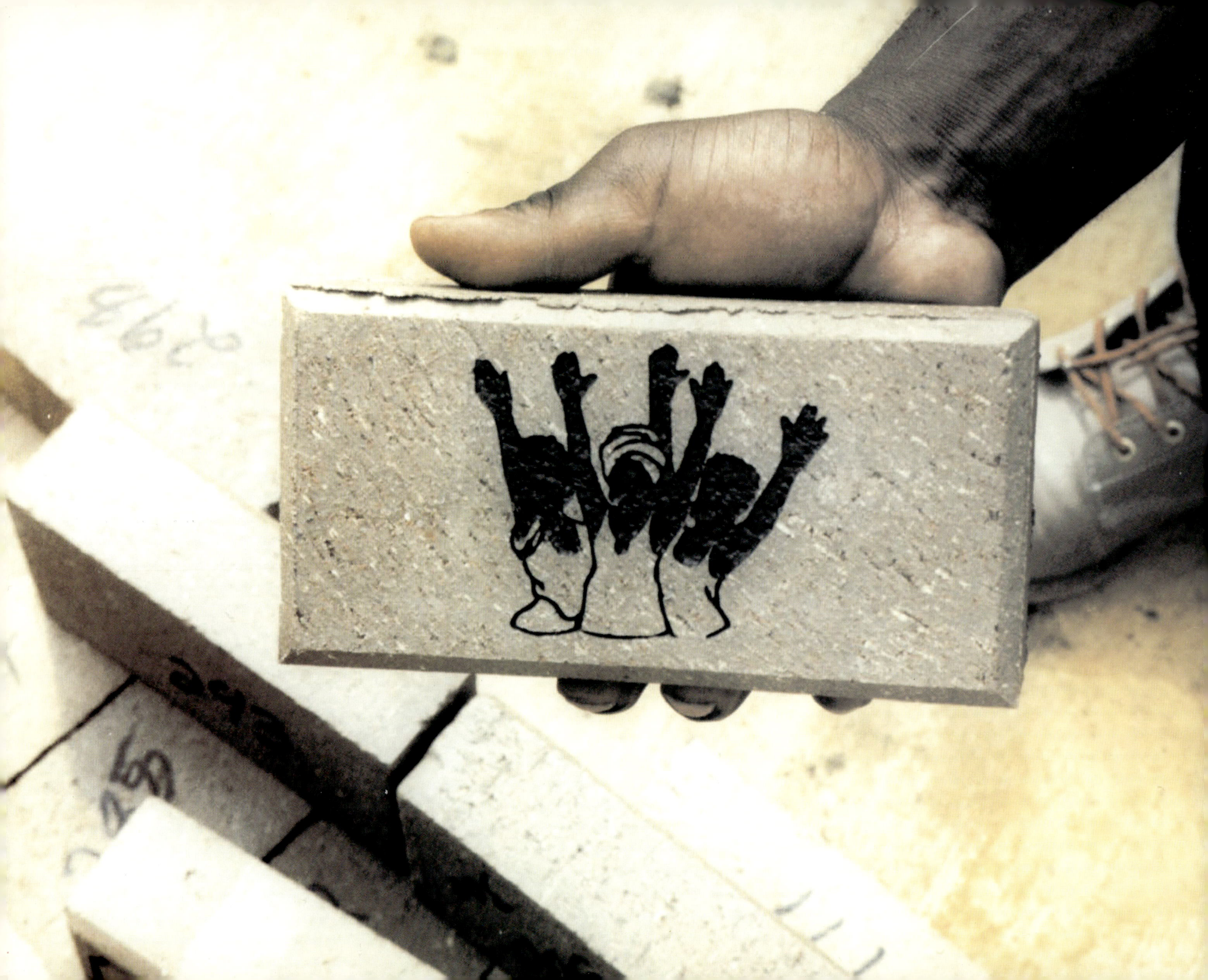

BRICK BY BRICK

...we built a wall.

In 2003 the "Sacred Wall" was erected as a permanent memorial in rememberance to the contributions and sacrifices Africans have made to all of humanity.

Pictured Left: The first brick unpacked for the Ancestral Sacred Wall is engraved with the WISOMMM logo.

Pictured Right: A close up of engraved bricks

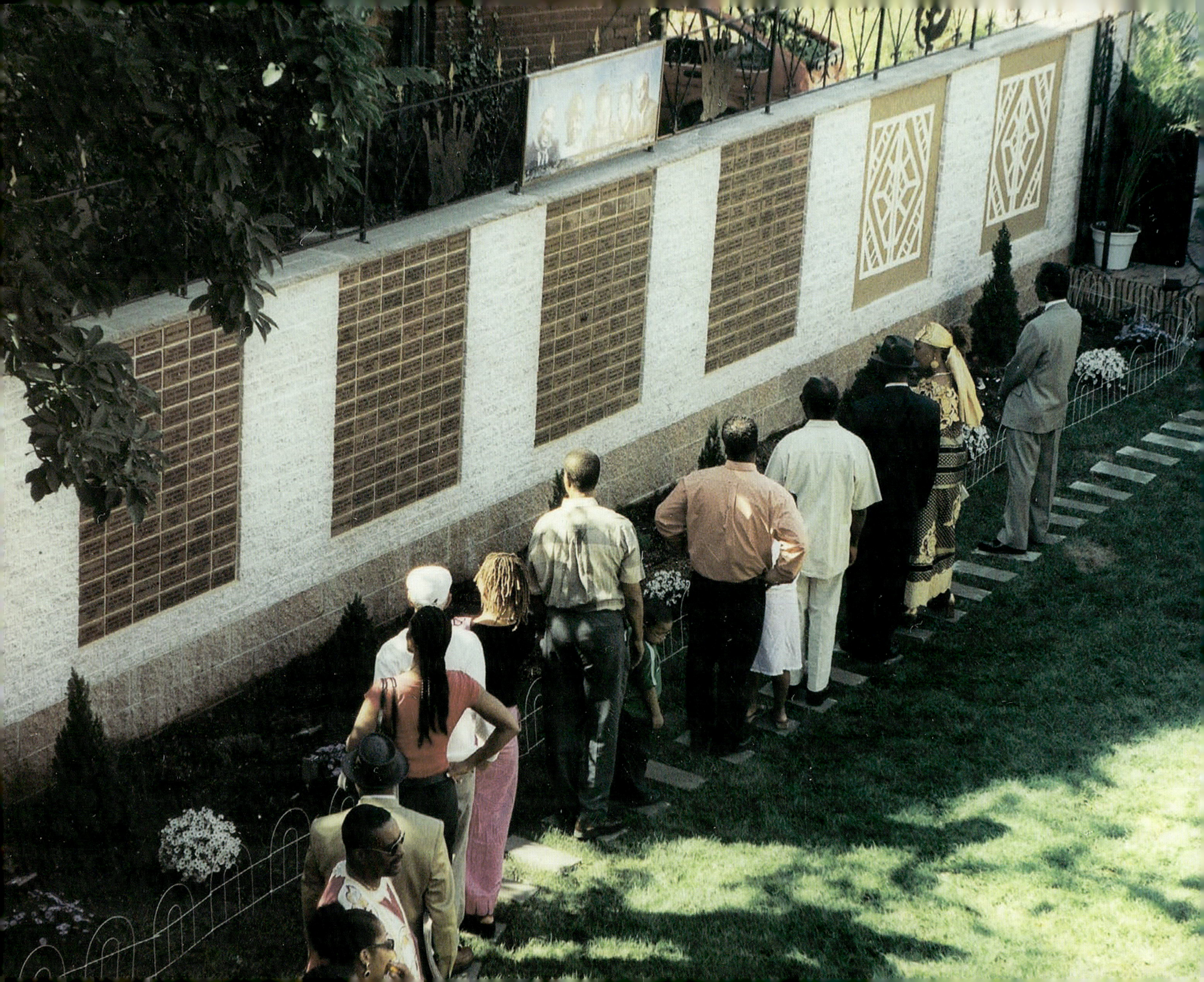

HONORING OUR ANCESTORS

For WISOMMM the unveiling of the Ancestral Sacred Wall in the Children's Garden was a momentous occasion.

The Sacred Wall is engraved with names of African families and prominent ancestors in African History. Brick by brick we pay tribute to those on whose shoulders we stand.

The Ancestral mural depicts the great "*Maafa*" (The great disaster) which spanned from Africa to Americas.

Pictured Left: Supporters of the Buy-A-Brick fund raiser read names engraved on the Ancestral Sacred Wall.

Pictured Right: Executive Board Member Audrey Chow-Jones unveils the Ancestral Mural in the WISOMMM Children's Garden. The mural is the work of Board Member Yvonne Onque and two of her sons, Samad and Sulaiman. The mural depicts the history of the African experience.

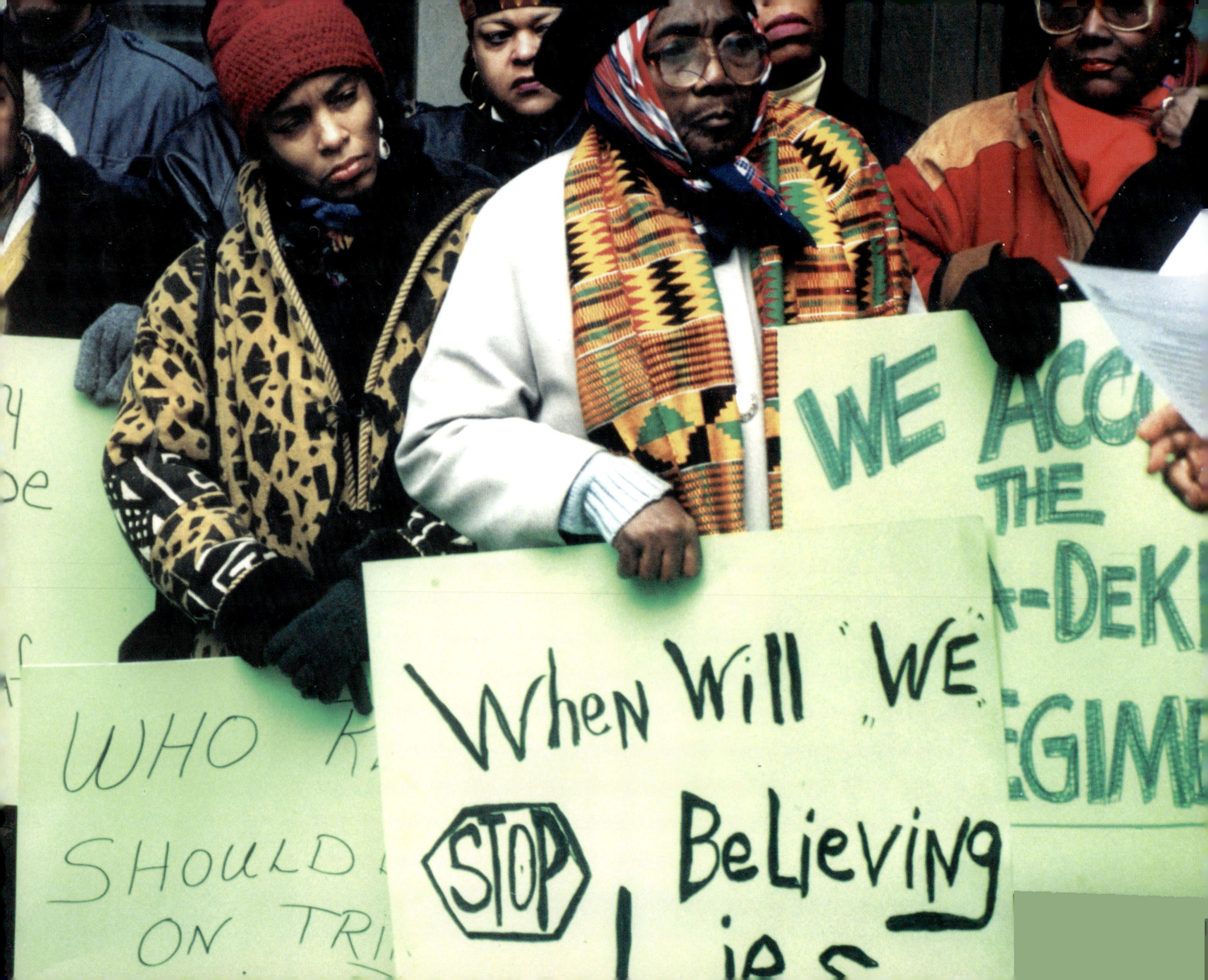
When Will "WE"
STOP
Believing
WE
THE
WHO
SHOULD
ON

WOMEN IN SUPPORT OF A FREEDOM FIGHTER

In 1999 WISOMMM shared the distinct privilege wtih Black Cops Against Police Brutality (BCAP) to co-sponsor a celebration in honor of South Africa's Queen Mother, Nomzamo Nobandla Winifred Mandikizela Mandela (Winnie Mandela).

Support for Sister Mandela has continued. WISOMMM joined forces with BCAP, Frontline Artists and The Committee to Eliminate Media Offensive To African People (CEMOTAP) in protest of negative propaganda during Winnie's "alleged" murder trial.

Pictured Left: Board Member Yvonne Onque and the late Professor Jeanette Cascone (right) are joined by other supporters of Winnie Mandela in front of the South African Consulate in New York City.

Pictured Right: Sister Winnie Mandela addresses the audience at BCAP's annual Pre-Kwanzaa celebration.

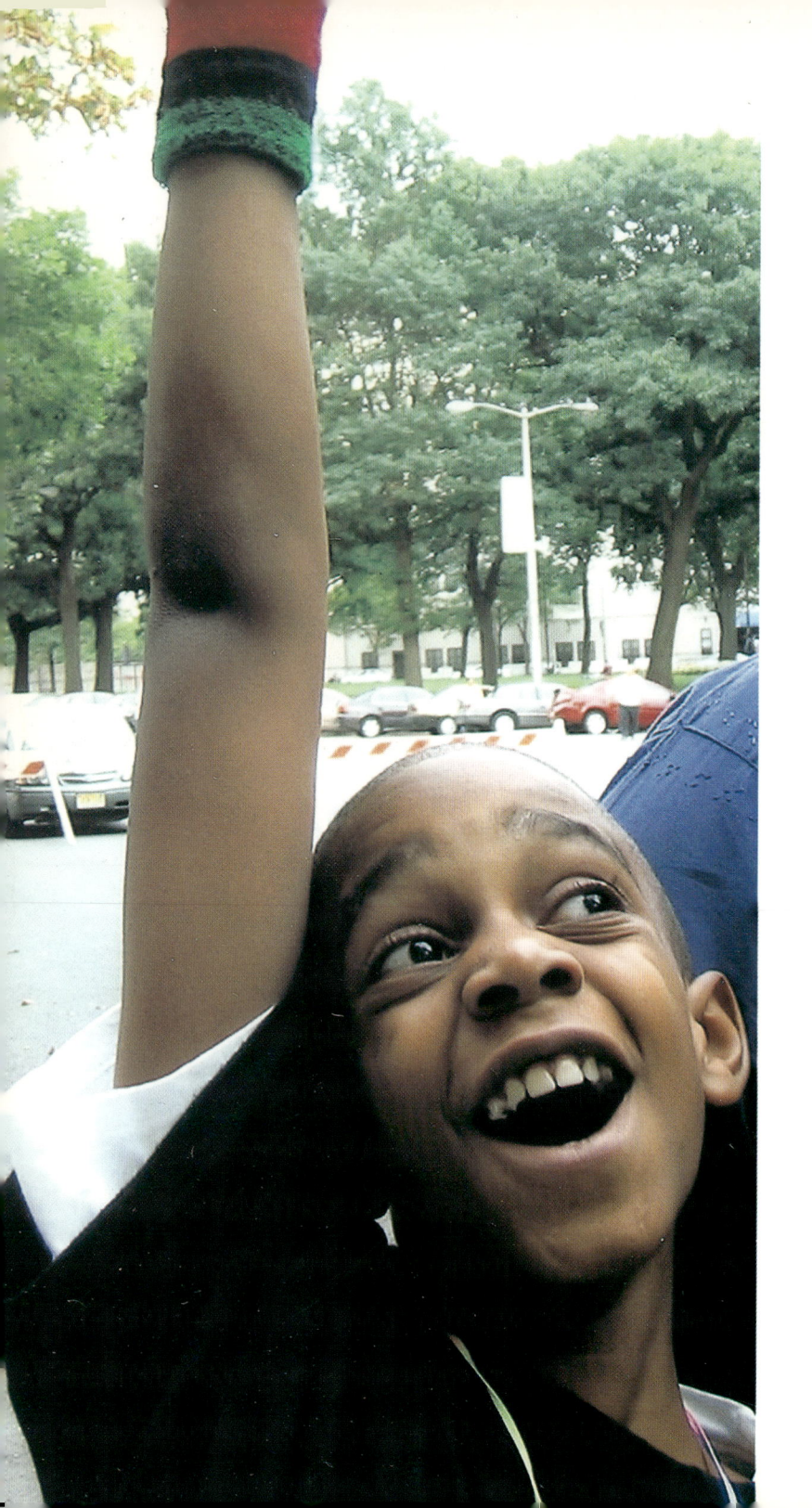

RITES OF PASSAGE

Building responsibility and character in youth is the work of adults.

The S.T.E.P. young mens Rites of Passage program means **S**triving **T**ogether **E**quals **P**rogress.

S.T.E.P. and various other programs are part of the WISOMMM family, each focused on helping youth grow into positive and productive adults.

Pictured Left : A member of the S.T.E.P. Male Rites of Passage program enjoys himself at WISOMMM's Annual Youth Festival. The young men of S.T.E.P. also perform martial arts as part of the youth showcase.

Pictured Right: Bro. Kenyatta Kenyatta (right) stands in formation with the young men of S.T.E.P.

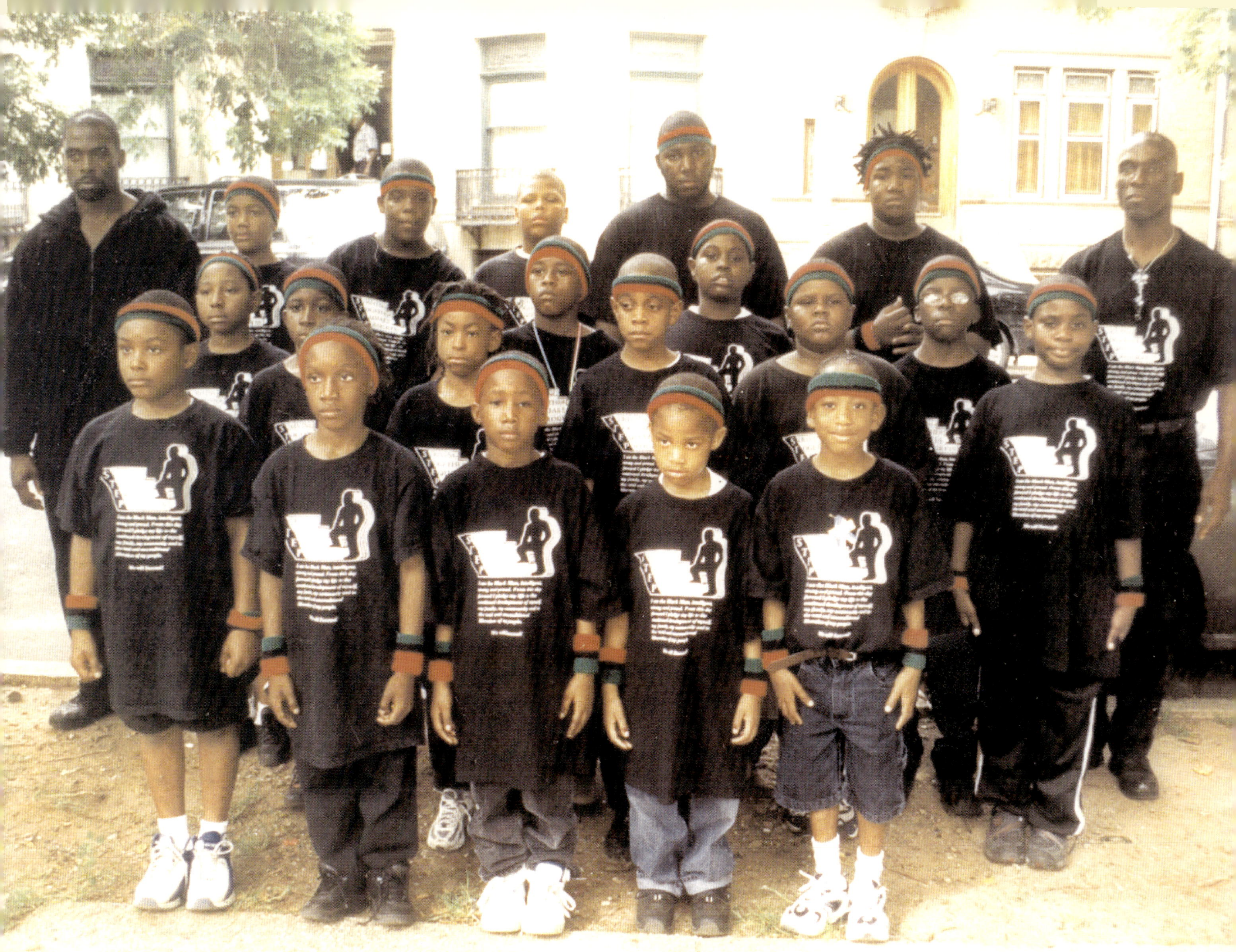

FUN FILLED FESTIVAL

Each year in September WISOMMM sponsors a free Back To School Youth Festival, a fun filled event that showcases the talents and aspirations of local youth.

Pictured Left and Right: Children and parents enjoy a day of fun and entertainment at the Back To School Youth Festival

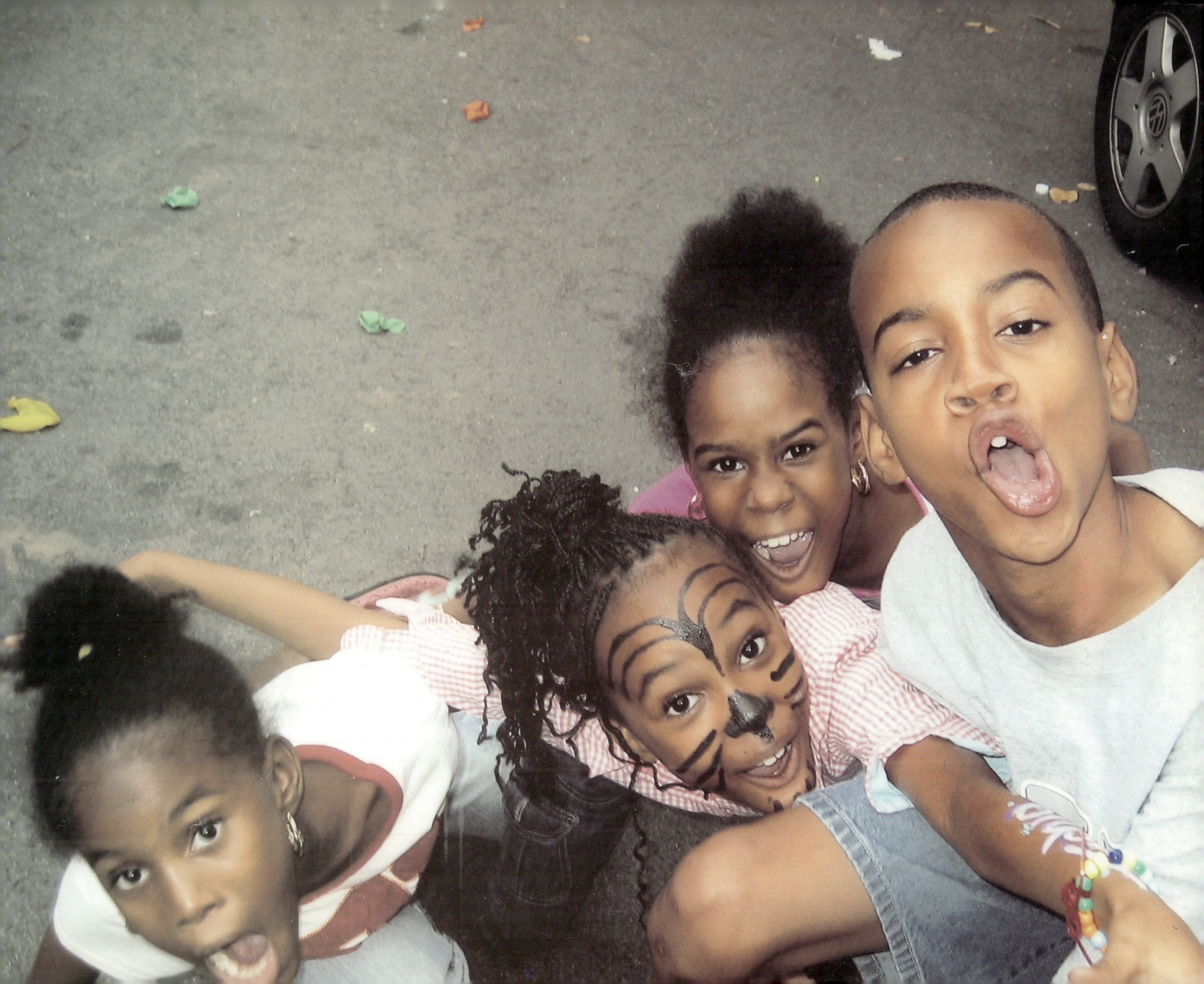

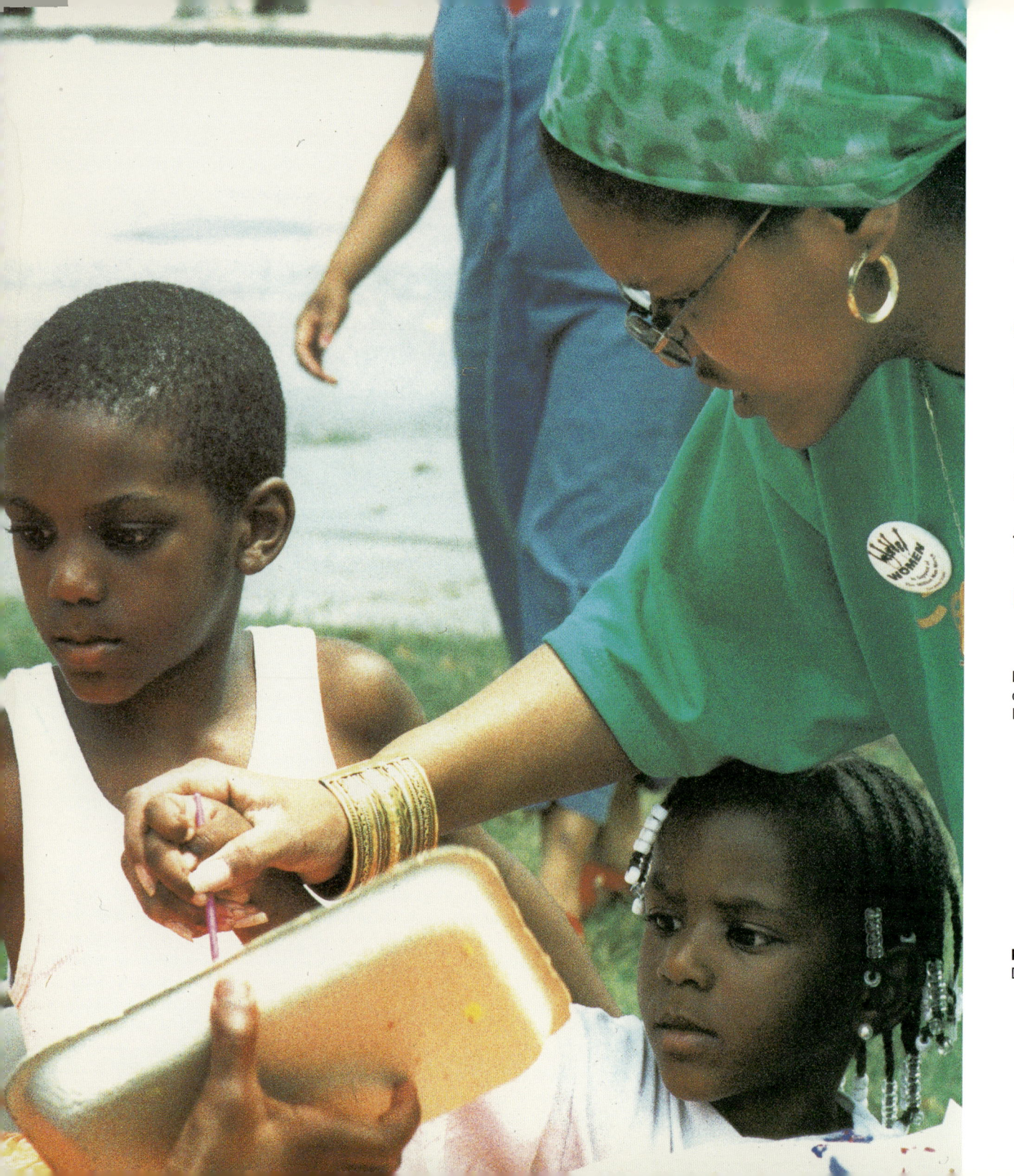

Talent shows, arts and crafts, essay and poetry contests, along with other positive youth activities bring kids and ther families together to share food, music, and fun.

Pictured Left: Board Member Hassana Shaw assists children who enjoy the arts and crafts at the annual Youth Festival.

Pictured Right: Executive Co-Chairwoman Professor Daphne Benyard painting faces.

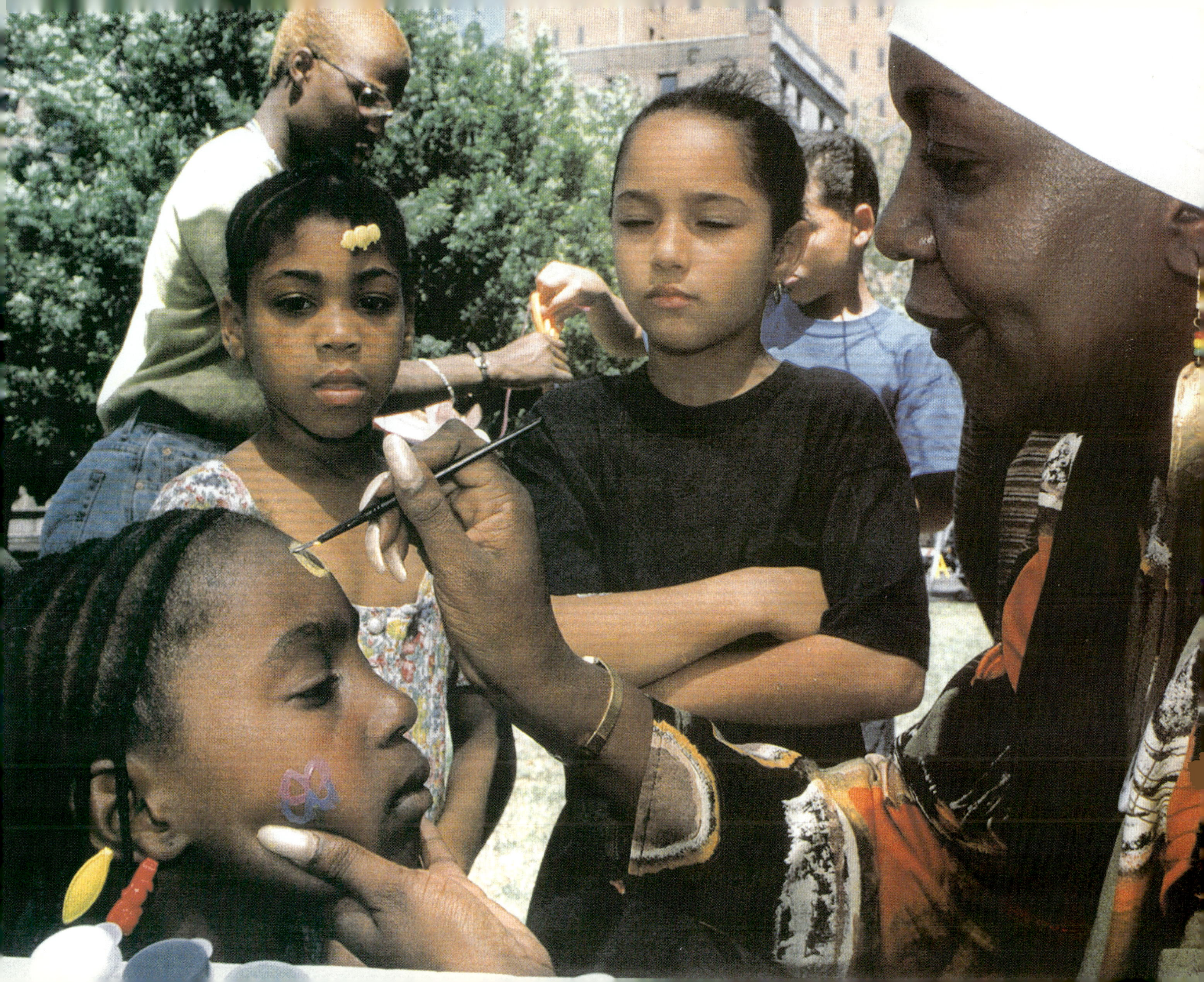

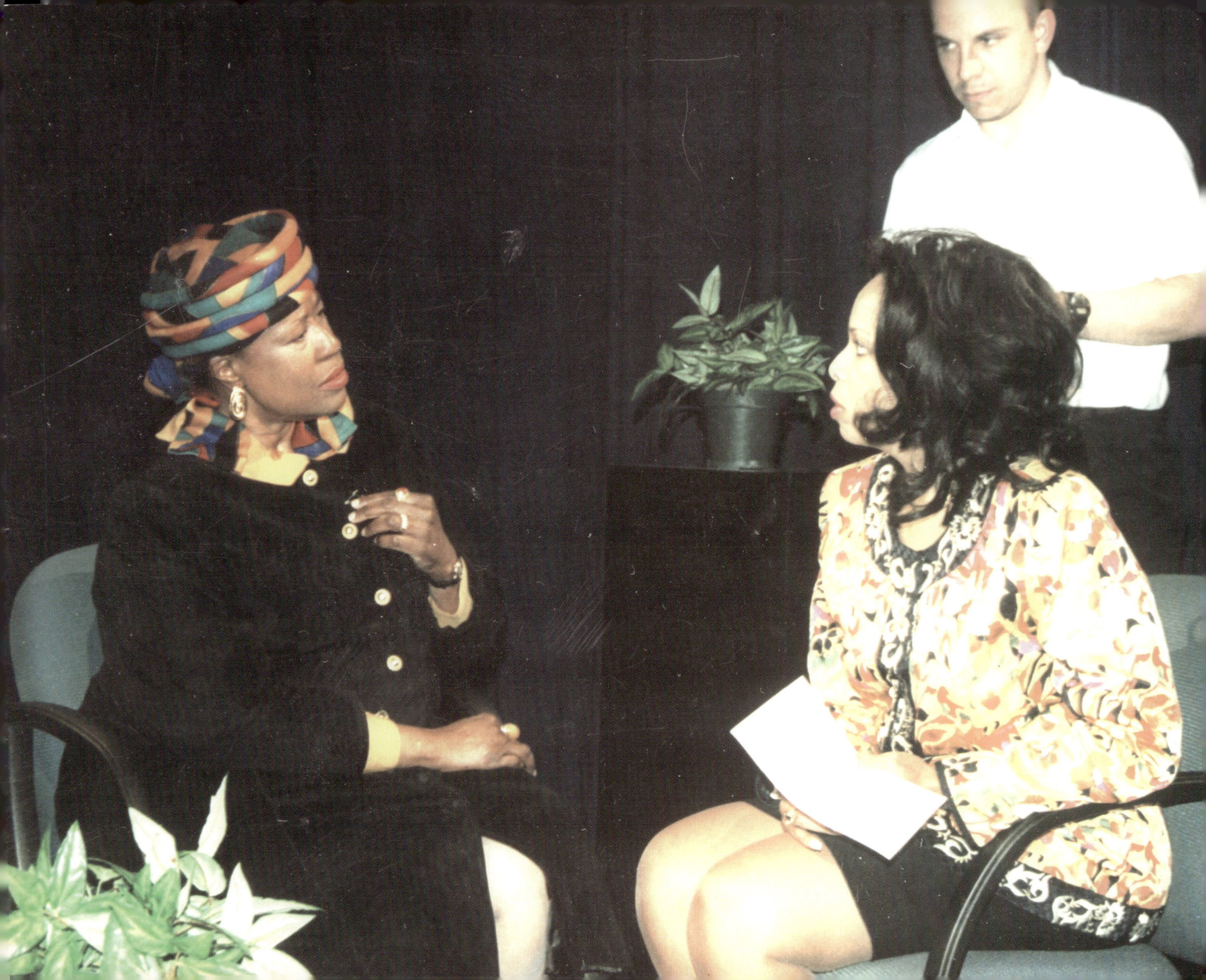

TELLING OUR STORY

Creating a positive image is vital to the success and capacity of any organization. WISOMMM tells its story in various ways: networking with other organizations, via the public access cable TV show, on the WISOMMM website, at public forums or in the WISOMMM newsletter. Either way having control of your information base is an absolute must.

Pictured Left: Fredrica Bey and Board Member Iry Harris hosts WISOMMM's first public access Cable TV Show.

Pictured Right: Fredrica Bey interviews Awardees Drs. Rosalind and Leonard Jeffries at the annual African Ball. Each year the ball is aired on the WISOMMM Cable TV Show.

THE BOYCOTT CRIME CAMPAIGN

The Boycott Crime Campaign - programs and events focused on providing young people with educational, cultural and economic alternatives to crime.

Pictured Left: Fredrica Bey address the community at a Boycott Crime public forum. Sgt. DeLacy Davis of Black Cops Against Police Brutality moderates the forum.

Pictured Right Executive Board Members Fredrica Bey (center) and Gloria Valentine (right) are joined by WISOMMM Advisory Board Member Raisah Myers.

The Boycott Crime Campaign was launched in October, 1998 by a group of concerned citizens and elected officials in Newark, NJ and other surrounding cities. The initial intent of the campaign was to serve as a "wake-up call" to urban communities in particular and to all people in general, to refrain from any and all activities or behavior that could be considered "criminal" and subject to inevitable short or long-term prison sentences.

MUM
STO
RACIST PO
BRUTAL
FREE
MUMIA
STOP
RACIST POLICE
BRUTALITY
Int'l Action Center NYC 212-633-6646
PHILLY 215-724-1618 www.mumia2000.org
MAAFA
ABU-JAM
ENT!
IF MU
DIS

AMERICAN PRISONS FORUMS...

The American Prisons Hearing of Citizens is a series of open forums and town hall meetings held to discuss and lobby against the human rights violations within the Prison Industrial Complex, and work out remedies and solutions to the same.

Pictured Left: WISOMMM Board Member s Akiba Ismail (2nd from left), Yvonne Onque (center) and Ayo McMillian (2nd from right) are flanked by supporters of Mumia Abu Jamal at a spirited rally for his release in Philadelphia, PA.

Pictured Left: Fredrica Bey (seated left) discusses prison policy reform with Tamika Riley of (TRI Productions) and Sgt. Delacy Davis of (BCAP) at a meeting with the New Jersey Department of Corrections.

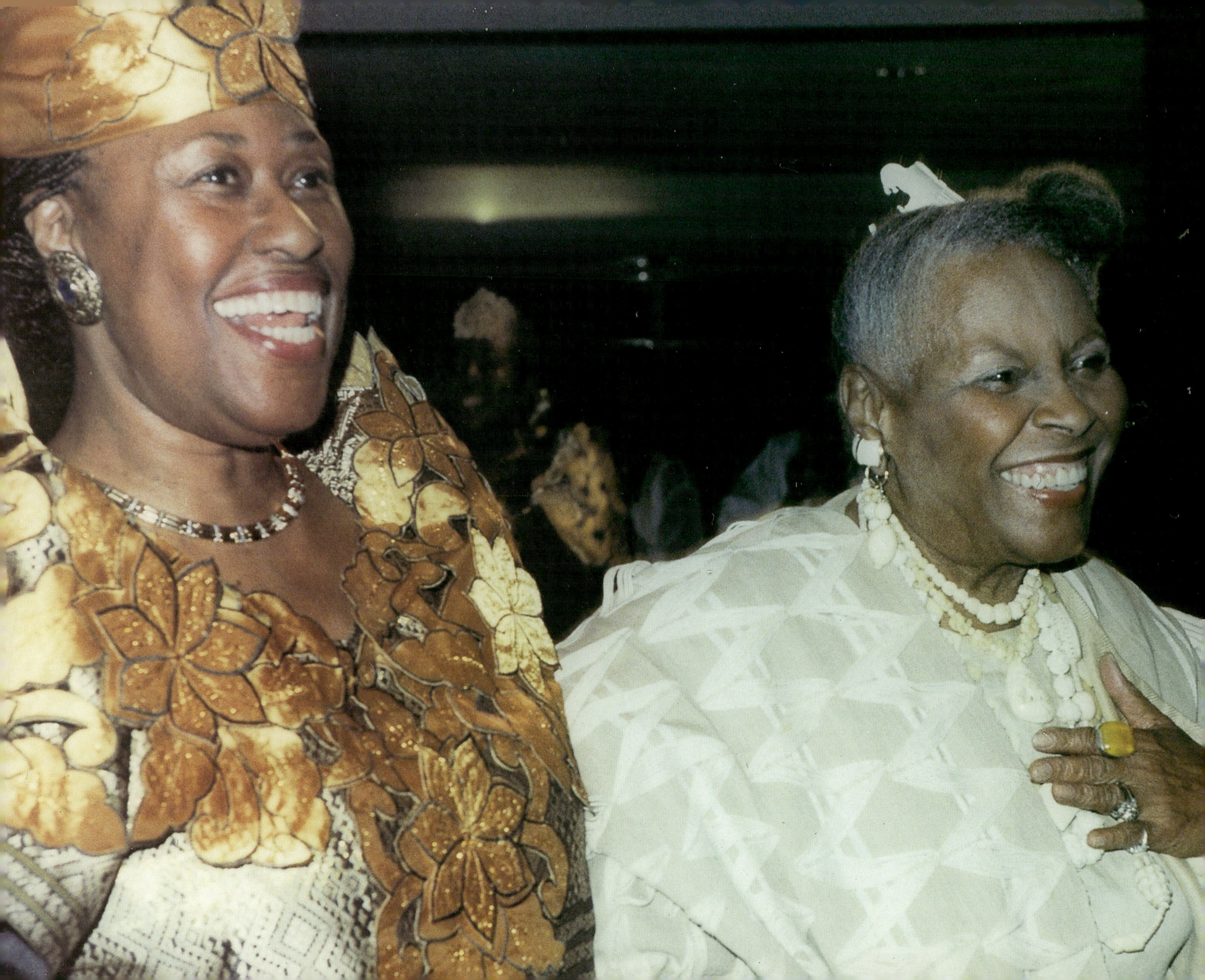

I AM BECAUSE WE ARE

WISOMMM has come to recognize the importance of "acknowlegement of self".

From within our community springs forth greatness of mind, body and spirit.

Pictured Left: Fredrica Bey escorts New York Board of Regents, Dr. Adelaide Sanford, 2003 Honoree for Lifetime Achievement. Dr. Sanford also serves on the WISOMMM Advisory Board.

Pictured Right: Board Member Tahirah Abdullah (center) escorts Jamillah and Ilyasin Muhammadi, 2002 Honorees for the Strong African Family Award.

Each year during the Fall the women of WISOMMM hosts an African Ball and Awards Dinner taking the opportunity to hold up brothers and sisters in the community who work to ensure the African continuum.

Whether through strong African families, entreprenuership, politics, education, arts and culture, community service or as an unsung heroes, these Africans are shining examples of the African genius that survived insurmountable odds.

Pictured Left: Vesta Godwin Clark, Chairwoman of the African Ball and Awards Dinner committee prepares the program for the evening.

The African Ball and Awards Dinner is just one of WISOMMM's annual events used to practice the Kwanzaa principles of "Kujichagulia" - Self Determination, and "Ujamaa"-Cooperative Economics.

The event highlights the achivements of the honorees and helps to fund the WISOMMM Holistic Child Care Center.

Pictured Right: Board Member Ayo McMilllian proudly looks on during the award ceremony. Ayo is also a member of the African Ball and Awards Dinner organizing committee.

FROM AN ORGANIZATION TO AN INSTITUTION

After a long and protracted, uphill struggle, and through the help of dedicated people the women of WISOMMM miraculously acquired a third historical property in Newark.

The Second Presbyterian Church at Newark, now known as the WISOMMM African Education and Cultural Resource Center (AECRC) is a 4.5 million dollar, 65,000 square foot multiple-complex located in Newark's Downtown district.

Pictured Left: The Second Presbyterian Church complex in Newark was purchased by WISOMMM on October 8th, 2004. Renamed the WISOMMM African Education and Cultural Resource Center, the facility has allowed the organization to expand existing programs, establish a for profit company and offer a community "home" that can hosts 2500 people at one event.

The **African Education and Cultural Resource** center is located in the northern portion of Newark's Central Business District on James and Washington Streets. It also lies in the James Street Commons Historic District. Immediate neighbors include The Newark Museum, the restored Ballantine House, the Newark Library, St. Michael's Medical Center, and numerous ground level stores, office towers, parking garages, restaurants and banks.

Other landmark properties include The New Jersey Performing Arts Center (NJPAC), Military and Washington Parks, Rutgers University, Rutgers and Seton Hall Law Schools, New Jersey Institute of Technology (NJIT) and Riverfront Stadium. Corporate neighbors include Verizon, IDT, Wachovia Bank, Horizon Blue Cross/Blue Shield and Public Service Electric and Gas Co.

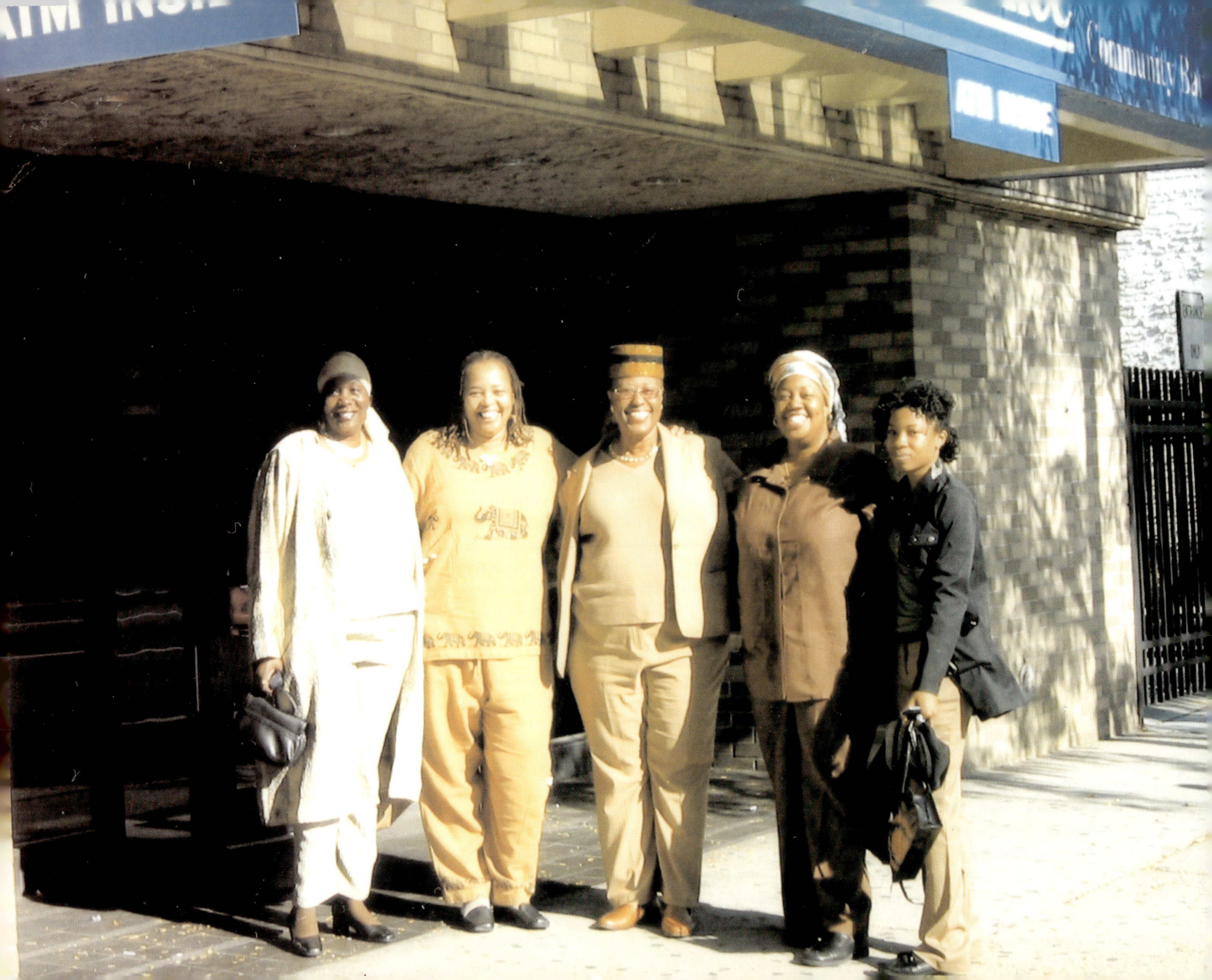
Community

WISOMMM finalized the purchase of the Presbytery at Newark on October 8, 2004 for $3,900,000. The property is comprised of three buildings (the Sanctuary, Hunter Hall and the Community Building), that have masonry walls of granite, brownstone and brick, has a total 65,180 square feet and a current appraised value of $5,000,000. The Center is the new home of the newly expanded WISOMMM Holistic Child Care Center, WISOMMM Event Services, (a community oriented banquet service) and the Boycott Crime Youth Program.

Pictured Left: WISOMMM Board Members prepare to enter the bank where they closed the $4.5 Million deal with Independence Community Bank.

Pictured Right: Executive Director, Fredrica Bey joyfully signs on the dotted line.

CELEBRATING OUR ACHIEVEMENTS

On December 4, 2005 joined by the community, WISOMMM celebrated the Grand Opening of Newark's first African Education and Cultural Resource Center.

Pictured Left: The Zawadi School of Drum and Dance lead the celebration for the Grand Opening of WISOMMM's African Education and Cultural Resource Center. Young ladies from the STARS Pageant (a positive self esteem program) graciously fill in as hostesses for the event. Both Zawadi and STARS are housed at the the cultural center.

Pictured Right: WISOMMM Board Members are honored by the community at the Grand Opening celebration.

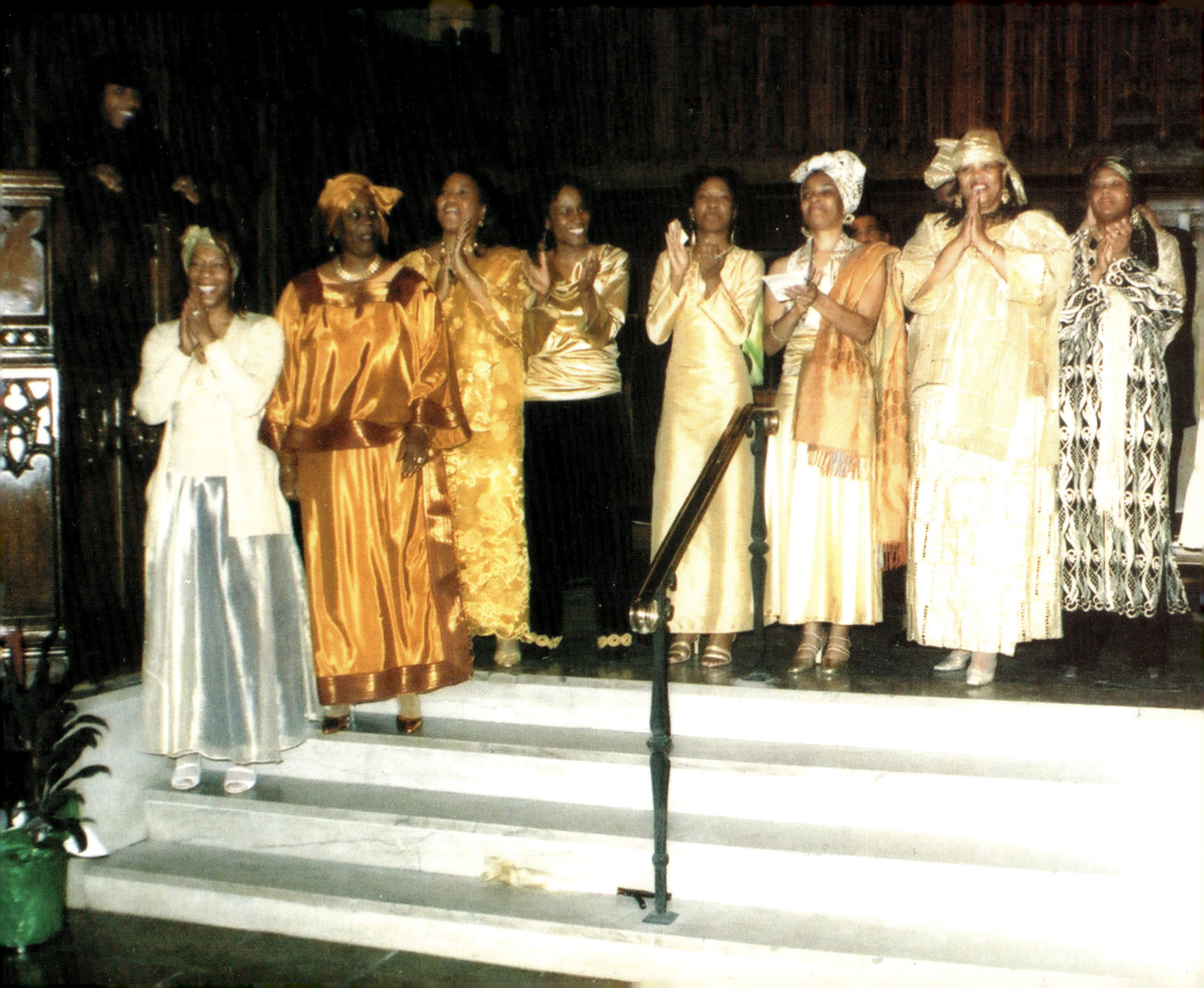

Fredrica Bey, WISOMMM's Executive Director, thanks Newark Mayor Sharpe James for his support. "We are a group of hard working sisters who receive a great deal of support from our Mayor. It was through his efforts, the efforts of Council Member Gayle Chaneyfield-Jenkins, Drs. Leonard and Rosalind Jeffries, Sy Hendrson, Ted Williams and so many other brothers and sisters in the community who helped bring us to this point. We thank Almighty God for allowing us to be a vehicle through which this work is done. We just pray that our Ancestors are proud and continue to give us strength and guidance to keep on keepin' on."

Pictured Left: *Newark's Mayor Sharpe James and gospel vocalist Joshua Nelson celebrate Dr. Martin Luther King, Jr's birthday in the WISOMMM African Education and Cultural Resource Center.*

Pictured Right: *Sy Henderson, WISOMMM's financial consultant, Dr. Adelaide Sanford and Sister Betty Dobson of CEMOTAP celebrate the Grand Opening of the WISOMMM African Education and Cultural Resource Center.*

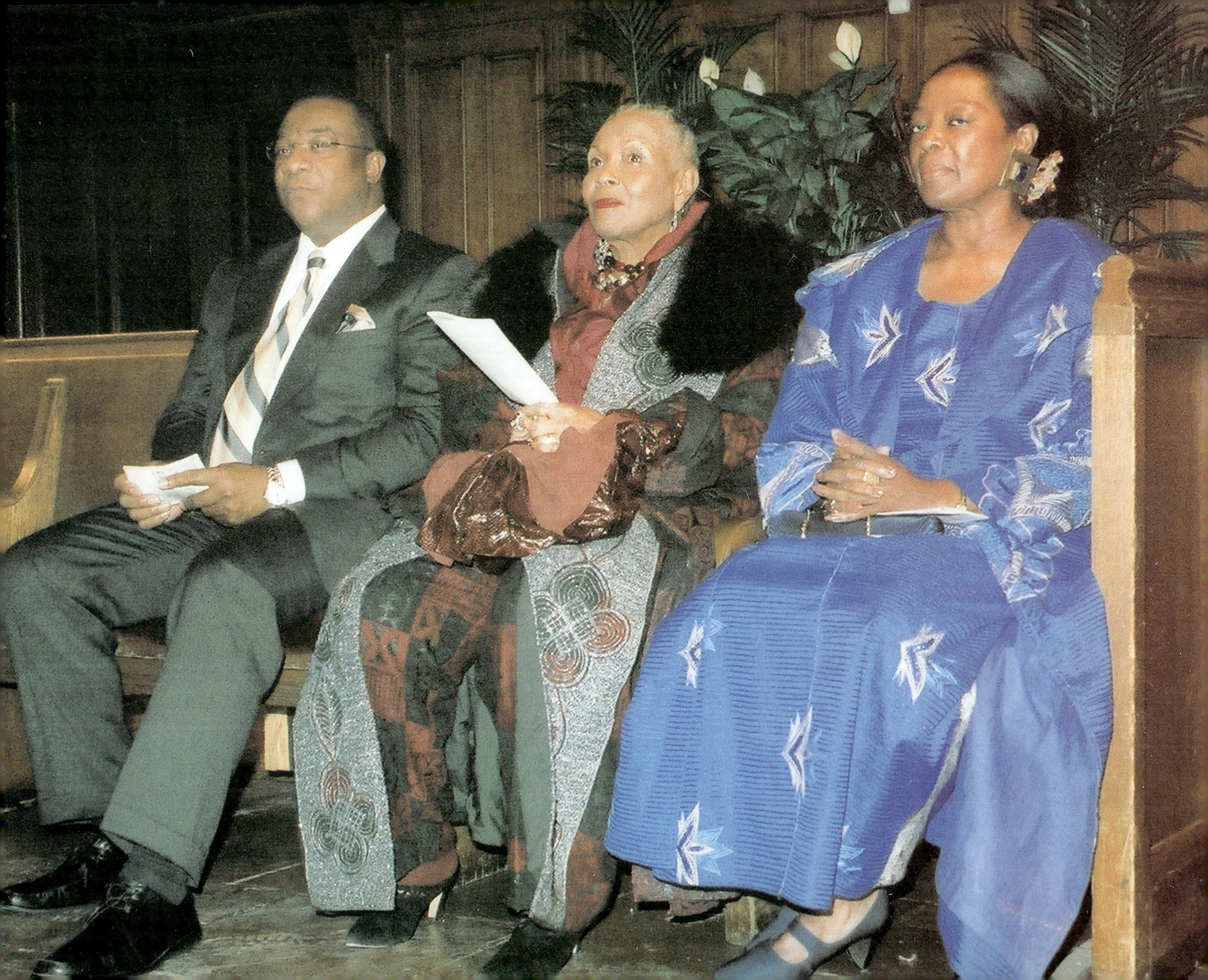

IT'S SO GOOD TO HAVE A MAN AROUND THE HOUSE

WISOMMM began in support of men. Many of those men have rallied around the Women of WISOMMM in love and support.

Rayford Scott of Kindle and Scott Contractors has almost single handedly renovated both WISOMMM Mansions I and II. He tirelessly continues to work, often volunteering his time.

Pictured Left: *Co-Chairwoman Aminah Bey proudly looks on as her step-father Rayford Scott receives a much deserved appreciation award from the women of WISOMMM.*

The Million Man March celebrates its 10th anniversary in October, 2005

WISOMMM proudly joins the over two million men and their families in another historical celebration.

WE SALUTE OUR BROTHERS

Other WISOMMM Brothers...

DELACY DAVIS, DR. LEONARD JEFFRIES, FAHEEM RA'OOF, SY HENDERSON, WILLIAM FRAZIER, JOHN HOWARD, RENARD SCOTT, ANTHONY SCOTT, YUSEF ISMAIL, RAFAEL MENA, DR. JAMES McINTOSH, MALIK AKBAR, SULAIMAN ONQUE, SAMAD ONQUE, RASHID ONQUE, TED WILLIAMS, LARRY LAWSON, SAADIQ SHAKOOR, FAHEEM SALAAM, MIN. AKBAR MUHAMMAD, MIN. MICHAEL MUHAMMAD, MIN. KADIR MUHAMMAD, CAPTAIN MAJEED MUHAMMAD, MIN. LAWRENCE MUHAMMAD, MIN. JAMEEL MUHAMMAD, ABDUL MATIN UMAR, PHILIP THOMAS, BILL HINES, RON TOLIVER, GREGORY JONES, RODNEY MUHAMMAD, and all of the Brothers of Integrity and Port Houses.

Pictured Right: Mr. William Frazier, a strong WISOMMM brother, photographer and member of the WISOMMM Advisory Board

A CALL ANSWERED

in 1995 the Honorable Minister Louis Farrakhan, leader of the Nation of Islam called for a milllion black men to assemble in Washington, DC. Nearly two milllion men answered his call.

WISOMMM also answered the call and recommited themselves to the message of atonement and reconciliation to The Creator, to families and community.

The women of WISOMMM have had the honor of hosting Minister Farrakhan on several occasions. During these visits he shared his wisdom, advice and pledge of support.

Pictured Left: *Minister Louis Farrakhan, Spiritual Leader of The Nation of Islam is interviewed at WISOMMM's African Education and Cultural Resource Center.*

The Women In Support of the Million Man March are joined by the Honorable Minister Louis Farrakhan to celebrate the opening and dedication of the WISOMMM African Education and Cultural Resource Center.

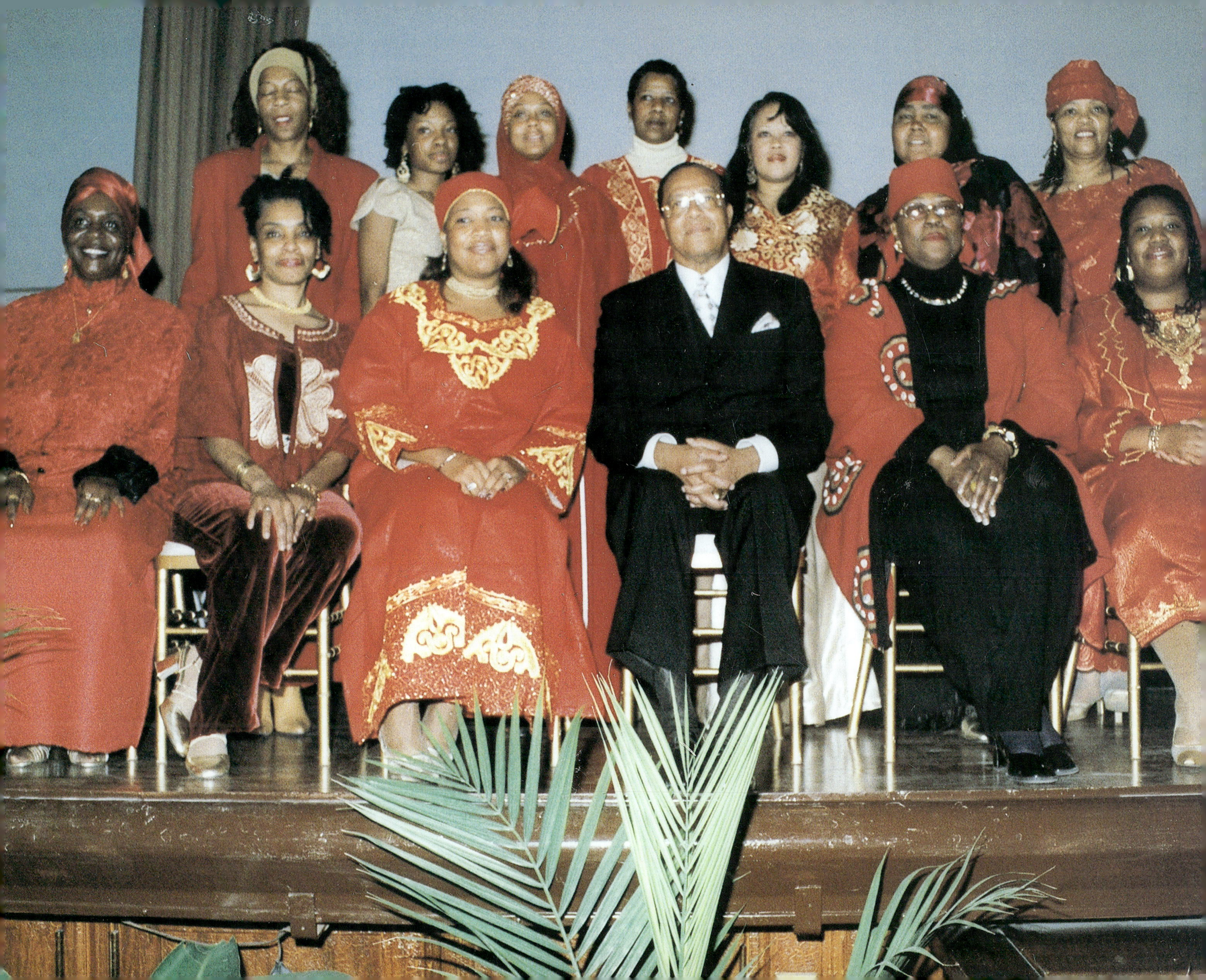

A GRAND QUEEN

Sister Fredrica Bey's determination has made WISOMMM one of the foremost respected and powerful organizations in the State of New Jersey.

Her vision and magnanimous heart is what guides the force of WISOMMM.

In May 2005 Sister Bey regally served as one of the Grand Marshals for Newark's African American Heritage Parade.

Pictured Left: *Executive Director Fredrica Bey addresses spectators of the African American Heritage Parade. Ms. Bey was honored as Co-Grand Marshall along with Newark dignitary Calvin West.*

Pictured Right *Board Members Charlotte Munnerlyn and Bonita Satterfield carry the WISOMMM banner at the African American Heritage parade*

WOMEN IN SUPPORT OF THE
MILLION MAN MARCH, INC.
WISOMMM, INC.
PARK
Women In S
of the
Million Man

WISOMMM 10 YEAR HIGHLIGHTS

1995 *Funded and rallied over 50,000 men into Washington, DC from NJ to the historic Million Man March*

1996 *Formed a non-profit corporation - WISOMMM, Inc.*

1997 *Fund raised to and purchased the WISOMMM Mansion at 53 Lincoln Park*
Sponsored First Annual Children's Arts Festival
Girls Scouts of Greater Essex and Hudson Counties became residents of the WISOMMM Mansion
Muslim, Inc. became residents of the mansion
Newark Teachers Association became residents of the mansion
Opening of the children's Math and Science Academy
WISOMMM Computer Lab opens
Launched WISOMMM Banquet Services
Honorable Louis Farrakhan visits the mansion
Hosted Interfaith Pilgrimage which retraced the African Slave Trade route from America to Africa

1998 *Launched quarterly "American Prisons...Second Coming of Slavery" Public Forum*
Founded Boycott Crime Campaign
Hosted monthly meetings of Sisters Network Breast Cancer Support Group
Produced the WISOMMM Cable Television Program

1999 *Co-Hosted Winnie Madikizela Mandela at a grand reception*
Joined Newark's Lincoln Park Arts Corridor Committee

2000 *Child Care Center under construction at 53 Lincoln Park*
Launched the WISOMMM website - www.wisommm.com

2001 *Opened The WISOMMM Child Care Center*
Purchased 67-69 Lincoln Park, Newark, NJ - A second mansion
Isaiah House's HIV/AIDS Counseling Program, residents of the mansion
Board Members attended the International World Conference on Racism

2002 *Coordinated community anti-gang violence coalition*

2003 *Erected a sacred memorial wall to African ancestors who perished during the middle passage*

2004 Purchased the 2nd Presbyterian Church at 15 James Street to develop Newark's first African Education and Cultural Center
Co-sponsored Black Cops Against Police Brutality 13th annual Pre-Kwanzaa Fest

2005 Expanded WISOMMM Child Care Center
Established WISOMMM Event Services a for profit subsidiary
Returned to Washington, DC for the Millions More Movement
Relaunched the WISOMMM website--www.wisommm.org

WITH HELP FROM OUR FRIENDS

With much guidance from the Ancestors WISOMMM has dispelled the negative myths that Africans, women in particular are unable to work together.

It has been a miraculous journey but not without hundreds of supporters who have held together even in times of dispair.

Pictured Right: Fredrica Bey (seated right) and Regent Adelaide Sanford enjoy a day of networking between two sister groups. Regent Sanford is a member of the New York based ISIS Sisters. Throughout the day both groups expressed the importance of "unity".

WISOMMM BOARD MEMBERS

PAST and PRESENT

Fredrica Bey	Tahirah Abdullah
Yvonne Onque	Malika Shaw
Ayo McMillian	Fatima Rahim
Aminah Bey	Hassana Shaw
Akiba Ismail	Keri Muhammad
Audrey Chow-Jones	Iry Harris
Daphne Benyard	Yvonne Hogan
Vesta Godwin Clark	Lola Harps
Bonita Satterfield	Gail Willis
Fatima Hafiz	Safiyya Sharif
Gloria Valentine	Lula Salvador
Charlotte Munnerlyn	Ruby Shivers

Fredrica Bey	Yvonne Onque	Ayo McMillian	Aminah Bey	Akiba Ismail	Audrey Chow-Jones
Daphne Benyard	Vesta Godwin Clark	Bonita Satterfield	Gloria Valentine	Fatima Hafiz	Charlotte Munnerlyn
Tahirah Abdullah	Malika Shaw	Fatima Rahim	Hassana Shaw	Keri Muhammad	Iry Harris
Yvonne Hogan	Lola Harps (Ancestor)	Gail Willis	Safiyya Sharif	Lula Salvador	Ruby Shivers

Conclusion

When the annals of the City of Newark are written recounting the significant achievements of the early 21st Century, the amazing accomplishments of the Women in Support of the Million Man March (WISOMMM) will be featured prominently.

It is testimony to their pioneering spirit that in a society where the accomplishments of women are often overlooked WISOMMM would emerge from the Million Man March leading the way for a revolutionary change in the educational, cultural, spiritual, and business life of New Jersey, and indeed the world.

Their impact on the redevelopment efforts currently underway in the historic Lincoln Park and historic James Street Districts of Newark is unrivaled by any other single entity. And this is just the beginning.

With their most recent acquisition of the historic Second Presbyterian Church a significant stabilizing force has taken root.

The wide range of programs planned in the African Education and Cultural Resource Center will address the needs of the indigenous community residents in the neighborhood.

This is a lofty ideal to pursue, but an attainable vision whose outcomes we can all embrace. It is in our hands.

Philip Thomas
Performing Arts Service